Charley

The First Year of a Standard Schnauzer

c.f. lutz

Plum Island
COMMUNICATIONS
Newburyport, Massachusetts

ISBN: 0692160310
ISBN-13: 978-0692160312

Published by:
Plum Island Communications
Newburyport, Massachusetts

This book, as well as my life, is dedicated
to my wife, Pat, without whom I would
only have managed to dream of happiness.

And our soul mates:

Queenie
Taffy
Sheba
Gunther
Tiffany
Twain
Holly
Lucy

and of course
Charley

ACKNOWLEDGMENTS

A huge hug to mom, also known as Pat Lutz,
my beautiful wife and the owner and teacher at
The Artists Playground, Newburyport, MA

Pat converted all of the photos into the color-able line drawings
that are in the back of the book.

I know it sounds like a cliché, but I really couldn't have done this
without her. She is my inspiration, proofreader, artist
and shining light, not to mention, love, of forty years!

We would also like to thank
Facebook
in general for just being there, and in particular, the

Standard Schnauzers Owners and Breeders Group

for their advice, encouragement and support.

Last, but really, first, thanks to
Shalimar's Standard Schnauzers
for being there to provide the best little girl
family member we could have hoped for.

CONTENTS

Dad & Charley

A much needed introduction:

Hi! My name, at least for the purpose of this book, is dad. Actually, it's not even a 'real' book. It's kind of a diary or notebook or journal but, no, not really any of those either. I think we will coin a new name for what this is. Of course, mom (another character in this 'not-book'), Charley and I have hashed this over extensively and we are finally going with Charley's idea. We are calling this a '*Pupette*'!

I know, I know, weird, right? Please do not pre-judge. Once you begin to read I am certain you will wholeheartedly agree with any description that borders on or even epitomizes, weird!

This all began to take shape when mom and I drove to a place called Shalimar's Standard Schnauzers, a breeder in Angola, NY. It was a 12 hour drive each way but it was well worth it because we were meeting our new family member, Charley. She was born on September 1st and would be 9 weeks old on November 3rd – and ready to go home with her new family.

When we met the breeder, Nonie Lomando, of Shalimar's, we found her to be all we would expect in a breeder. She was responsible, caring and informative. We were soon on our way home with Charley.

I had done a couple of Facebook posts on the way. All our friends were interested in our progress. But, once we got home and Charley realized she could communicate via Facebook, well, there has been no stopping her. One problem has been that she just writes 'stream of thought' so she isn't always grammatically correct. I have decided to leave things alone so you can appreciate all of her nuances.

As we begin this pupette, Charley is now 9 months old. I happen to be 73 years old wondering if I have finally, totally, lost my marbles. What am I doing with a puppy? I have had multiple spinal injections, 2 major back surgeries and they want to do another. I had both of my knees replaced a year ago and I get a needle in my eyeball every month. To top it off, I'm a recovered alcoholic (many years) and we manage (mostly Pat, my wife), a full time business, *The Artists Playground*, in Newburyport, MA, where Pat teaches all forms of art to adults and children. Good thing I married a younger woman! Of course, Pat says I am 73 going on 14!

Pat is right, I really am 'young at heart' and I absolutely believe you are as young as you feel. It also helps to pay much more attention to my spiritual, rather than my physical self. But, believe me, if you want to test this philosophy, have a 9 week old Standard Schnauzer join your family. And, yeah, for me, it's worth it!

Every once in a while you may find a reference to something that you don't have a clue what Charley is talking about. Just ignore it, sit back with some ice cream and a drink of your choice and keep reading. All of this book came from our Facebook site and sometimes we may have stuck some of dad's poetry or whatever before or after Charley's post. Also, you may see some references to videos, but I can't for the life of me figure out how to show them in this book. Alas, until we can print a book like The Daily Prophet in Harry Potter where a two dimensional page shows animated pictures, I'm afraid we are out of luck.

However, if you have a strong desire to see a video starring Charley, you are welcome to visit our Facebook page. It is: https://www.facebook.com/PlumIslandChuck .

Finally, as a little background about us, we live in a home that we lovingly call our "Plum Island Paradise". It is located on Plum Island, Newburyport, Massachusetts.

Our school website is: TheArtistsPlayground.com, where Pat writes an occasional blog at TheArtistsPlayground.com/blog.

Dad's website is: StepsToTheSpirit.com , where you can discover the strange fellow he is. Please enjoy the book!

CHAPTER 1
September & October 2017

A collage of Charley and her brothers & sisters.

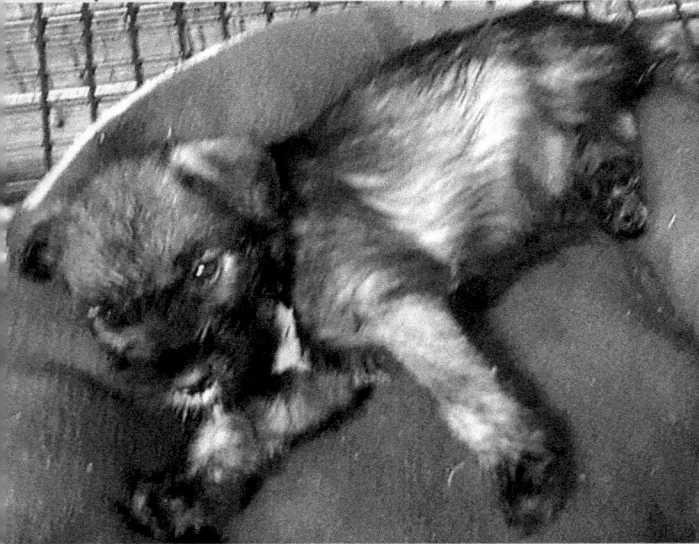

CHAPTER 2

Our tale begins in New York, just south of Niagra Falls. Charley was born on September 1st, 2017 and the breeder (Nonie) from Shalimar's Standard Schnauzers, likes the pups to stay with their litter and mom for 9-10 weeks. We had mixed feelings because it wasn't that long since we lost our Lucy but we love having a dog in our home. We were really lucky to find Charley. One breeder told us their next litter would be in 2020 and it was already sold out!

November 2, 2017

Here we are in Hamburg, NY, just south of Buffalo. It took us 10 hours to get here. The biggest holdup was getting from Newburyport to Boston ... 1½ hours!

Just spoke to the breeder a while ago and she will bathe Charley tomorrow morning and insert her ID chip. We will pick her up about 1:00 tomorrow and head home. Hope we get home before midnight!

Our room is nothing to brag about. When I lay on the bed it feels like I have my feet in a talk show and my head at the Daytona Five Hundred!

On the bright side, we had dinner tonight at a place next door called the *Water Stone Grill*. The food was the best either of us have had in ? years! Pat had a Chicken Marsala and I had Gorgonzola Sirloin with Pasta and Mushrooms. Incredible! And our server, Elaine, was delightful! And ... and ... we couldn't even take a doggie bag with us!

The WaterStone Grill was a very plesant surprise.

Oh, well, tomorrow is a new day and we can't wait to introduce you all to our newest family member.

We woke to the spectacular views of Hamburg, NY this cloudy, rainy morning. There are the rolling hills of asphalt and wildlife everywhere. We were lucky to see the Speeding White Trailer Beast and then (my heart be still) the rare Blue & White Move-Bird! We even caught a glimpse of the nearly extinct Wheeled Boxorus!!

Oh, well, our visual beauty will soon be history as we are off for breakfast at the famous 5 star Denny's and then ... and then ... oh yeah, we have to pick up that puppy!

The view from our room.

November 3, 2017

BUT ... the view inside our room was spectacular!! Pat is sitting in bed DRAWING! Well of course she is!
She has mixed emotions about the first, which is a pastel of our beautiful girl Lucy, recently gone ahead to wait for us in heaven.
The other is one of many, many samples she will be doing as visual aids for her upcoming watercolor class.
OK, Pat, put down the charcoal. It's time to get Charley!

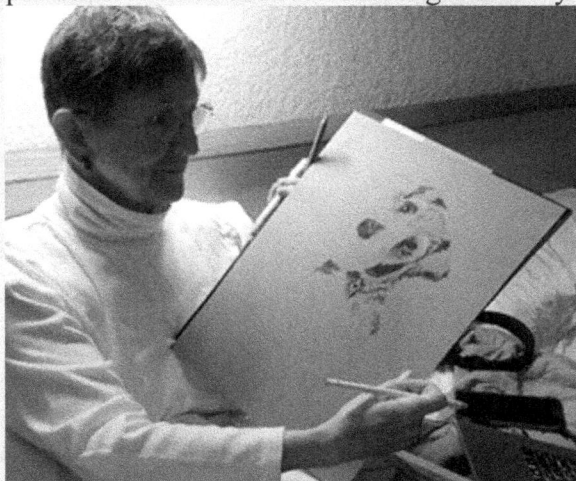

Lucy was the best – a true family member.

Pat is getting ready for a workshop.

November 5, 2017

Hey, Charley here! Just want to update you all. I finally met my new mom and dad. I've been practicing turning on the charm but it turned out I didn't need any. They seemed to immediately recognize that we belonged together.

I see dad already put our picture on the heading! He was so easy! And below, is mom and I when we met. We'll talk again soon!

"I found out mom's name is Pat."

"I found out dad's name is Chuck, but I like callin' them mom 'n dad"

November 5, 2017

Charley here again! They tell me I have a busy day ahead, meeting the family at my cousin Kate's party. And, I just saw a neighborhood future pal named Louie on FB!

But, right now, I want to set the record straight. There's a new top dog in town and I am tough as nails. But I'll let my actions speak for themselves. I have already had one intruder shaking in their boots until I realized it was dad testing me. Beware!!! (By the way, this was a video on Facebook. Just sayin'.)

November 6, 2017

Hi! Charley again!

As an update, my mom & dad seem to be adjusting to my way of doing things fairly well. They, on the other hand, said they are proud of me 'cause I haven't had this thing they call an accident. I don't get it. The pad is there ... you poop ... you pee ... finished. No worries!

I asked dad to take my photo so I can show you how I am doing. He says I am very fo-genic, whatever that means?

November 6, 2017

Charley again!
Dad decided to line up all my toys for a picture.
My breeder, Nonie, gave us a whole shopping
bag full of new toys!
p.s. Note from dad: When I let Charley out to
play with the toys, she walked past them all and
picked up the dead leaf.

Dead leaf!

November 7, 2017

Hi, Charley again. I hope you are not getting tired of my posts but I'm new at this and it's all very exciting! So, my breeder called again yesterday morning. I call her Nana Nonie, but don't tell her!! Well, she couldn't believe I went up the stairs at 9 weeks and asked if dad would video me. Here is a still from the video.

November 9, 2017

It's Charley again! So, tomorrow is going to be my 10 week birthday. But I'm not sure I'm feelin' it. I mean, I love mom & dad but man, they NEVER let up, especially him! It was sooo much easier and laid back in the litter. If I needed to pee or poop I could just let 'r rip. Even if one of the others was under it … not my problem. But now … now I have a TARGET. What do they think I am, a B-29? And, I tried puttin' my paws on it but no, no. I have to be concerned where my BUTT is positioned!

And all these RULES!!! Don't do this, don't do that, don't chew that, chew this squeeky pig lookin' thing instead. Oh, puh-leese, this is exactly why I said no to show business. Dad won't even let me chew on him anymore! OK, I'll admit the little hole in his nose was a bit too much but, hey, emphasis on 'little'!

Then, this afternoon I thought they said they were getting me some 'dark brillo' but it turns out I am going to see a Dr. Grillo. Hope he is nice. Maybe he is their shrink. God knows, they need one!

I may have to get some help. Can anyone out there hook me up with a Giant Schnauzer?

November 10, 2017

Charley here. Just a quick post tonight. I am totally exhausted 'cause dad had me playin' all day! Personally, I don't care much for the play stuff but I do it to make him feel good. Actually, I worry a little. How the guy even gets down on the floor, no less gets up, at 72 with 2 artificial knees, is beyond me. He even pretends to smile like he's likin' it. But, I brought him right back to reality with a little puncture wound in the earlobe.

Even so, he was nice when I asked him to take a pic to show me at my 10 week birthday. Here they are!

November 11, 2017

Charley here! It sure has been an adjustment at my new home. Don't get me wrong, it beats being packed in that litter with all those little nippers, like a bunch of pineapples. I'm the only little nipper now, although I have gotten the feeling that mom and dad would love to bite me back sometimes, especially dad.

It is hard for them to see my superior point of view. For instance, I wanted them to cut the legs off the furniture so I wouldn't lose my tennis ball, but noooo, they had a better solution as you can see below. Very funny dad. Do they think I'm a Great Dane? I could get a hernia with this thing! And I'm sure I saw a little smirk on mom's face.

The layout of the house is certainly not user-friendly to curious, fun-loving chewers like me. A lot of the time I'm stuck in the kitchen area and while it is big enough, I need MORE! They have these huge gates, like, 10 feet high! I'm sure they are afraid of something getting into the kitchen but I haven't seen it yet. My speed has helped because sometimes mom will open the gate to go through and close it and there I am, on the other side! Hee, hee! Bye for now. **"I'm not a GIANT Schnauzer!"**

November 11, 2017

NEWS FLASH BREAKING NEWS!!!

Charley again. Now they got this thing in the mail called a "Buddy Bowl". Warning to other pups out there ... it is NO FUN at all! It will not spill even if I tip it over! Geeeze!

November 12, 2017

I can't play right now, dad ... mom & I are talking about her slippers.

"Dad says that sometimes I don't have to write anything 'cause a picture is worth a thousand words."

November 12, 2017

But, cousin Kodi, I want to learn to be big and strong like you!

Sorry kid, you better put on a few pounds and do a few laps around the dog park. Come back in 6 mos. and maybe we'll talk.

Hi everyone, Charley here! Today was a big day! I got to go visit my cousin Kodi! I've heard a lot about him. Dad says Kodi could jump straight up and look him right in the eye. WOW! My dad must be at least 20 feet tall!

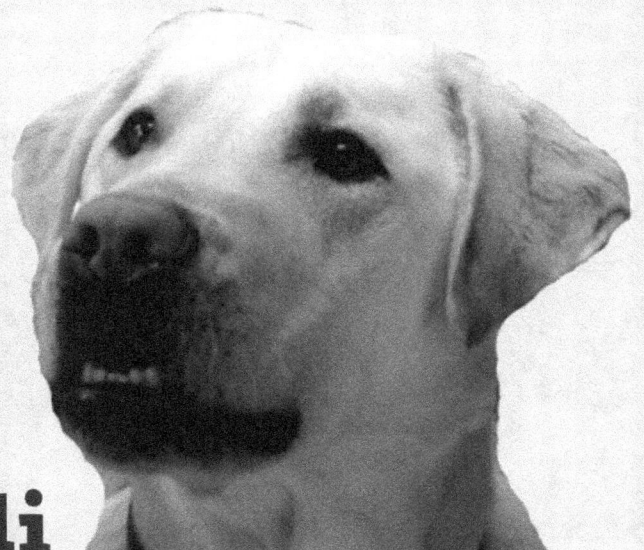

Kodi

Anyway, Kodi is a splendid hunk of animal, I mean, his tail is bigger than ME! I did all I could to impress him. I ran around the counters at full speed, doing my unique corner slides and tried to get up close and personal as, well, you know, only our kind can do! But he would have none of it and just wouldn't engage. Anyway, it was great to see him and, luckily, I'll get another chance to impress him at Thanksgiving!

November 13, 2017

Hey, Charley again. Seems like every day there is a new problem. Now I'm finding out I'm not the only cute canine in the house! So far I've found 2 more … one is hiding in the oven and the other one is in a duplicate room upstairs. They must be communicating in some way 'cause they are playing the same game to torment me. Every move I make, they imitate it! It's infuriating! (no reflection on you, dad)

I've got a plan for oven dog. I'm gonna poop and then he'll poop in the oven!! Then I'll get mom to ask dad for biscuits. Oven dog will succumb to his own tricks!!! Anybody have ideas for the other one?

Me (Charley) at about 2½ months.

November 14, 2017

Just a few random photos

These are worse than the stairs in Hogwarts!

MORE stairs!

Oh, sure, I'll come... if you'll play the theme from Rocky!

Dad! Are you SURE he's nice?

Some days are just really, really good, if you know what I mean!

I LOVE Kate!

November 15, 2017

Hey, Charley again. Dad took some more pictures today. He says he wants to record my growth. I feel like a tomato plant! Anyway, we are going to visit Dr. Grillo tomorrow for my 2nd puppy shot. I saw him last week and he said my puppy teeth were nice and sharp and that I weighed 8.2 lbs. I think I've gained a little but it's hard to tell being that I don't wear clothes. Maybe I can get dad to buy me a t-shirt. He has one that he wears because he thinks it intimidates me. It says 'Alpha Male'. I want one that says 'Beta Female'. He'll think it makes me a cute underling but I'll tell everyone it means Better Female!

We are still working on training and I must report that mom and dad are coming along just fine. Sure, they are a little slow but I am making allowances for their ages. Nighty night. I'll let you know how my vet does tomorrow.

November 16, 2017

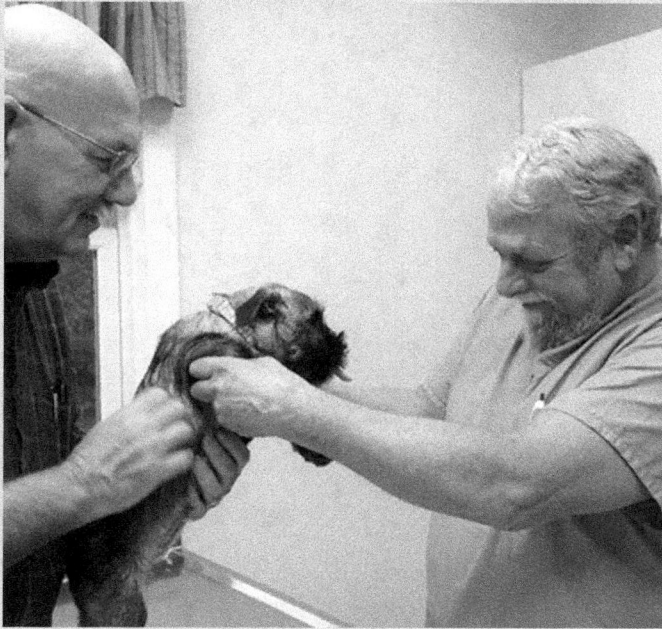

Hi everyone. It's Charley. Well, I had my visit with Dr. Grillo today and I thought it went well. First of all, I met Pamela in the parking lot and mom says she is my great-aunt. I think she is also related to Kodi so that makes her OK in my book. When we went in, there was a Westie and a Poodle already waiting and, I might add, getting a lot of attention. So, I put on my best puppy cuteness look and won everyone over. I think I heard someone say 'cutest pup that ever came through the doors of Newbury Animal Hospital', but I could be wrong about that. I think I saw an annoyed look from the Westie.

Then a gal brought us to the room. I tried to position myself in front of the scratch on dad's hand. Then, in comes Dr. Grillo. I met him last week and I like him a lot. Mom told me when we left that I got my shot! I didn't even realize it! He is GOOD! Now I feel bad that when dad asked if I should get more food and he said NO, I stuck my tongue out at him.

November 16, 2017

So, let me set the scene: dad is drivin' home from the vet, I am on mom's lap, they are chattin' away and laughin', "bet our little girl Charley will be pooped and sleepin' tonight!"
I 'rest' my case!

I think dad is gonna have to double up on his Ensure!

November 17, 2017

Hey, Charley again. Dad took me to Lowes today. We dropped mom off at Koh's and we went to get a key made and to buy a new heater. On the way in dad said Lowes is 'dog friendly' but on the way home he said it was too friendly. He told mom that what should have taken 10 minutes took an hour and I think I had something to do with it. It seemed like dad knew every person in the store! At least they all came over to say hi. Dad carried me cause he said my legs would go through the holes in the cart and everyone would think I was a baby seal or somethin'. Then the guy makin' keys told dad all about when he was a mini schnauzer breeder. Then dad had some fun when an elderly lady walked up to us and said, "what a cutie-pie"! Then, with a little wink, dad said, "why, thank you! And what do you think of my puppy?"

But, I think the last straw was when we were leavin' with the big heater and some guy asked dad if he needed help. Dad said no thanks and the guy said it was OK, he really just wanted to see his puppy! Anyway, here are some 11 week photos.

November 18, 2017

OMG, everyone (I learned that from a gal who wrote to me)! Today has been the worst day of my life! It was even worse than the day they snipped off my tail (and a little too short, I might add). For the first time, dad went off on errands without me! Mom said there were just things he had to do, you know, human things, and I just wasn't quite old enough to help this time. Dad actually gave me quite the hug before he left (I'm glad I already pooped after lunch) and I could tell he was gonna miss me too. There's somethin' you have to understand about us Standard Schnauzers. We live to bond with and protect our families. Don't put us out in the yard. Oh, no. We want to be at your feet, in your face and sometimes, under your butt when you try to sit down. So you can imagine how shaken I was when dad left. Mom tried her best to sooth me and our bond got even tighter. Of course, the popcorn and pet-icures for us gals didn't hurt either! But I sure was happy to see dad open that door. I almost licked off his mustache. And he said he was thinkin' of me 'cause he bought me a chicken flavored bone. What a mom & dad I have!

Bye, dad. I miss you already!

Mom! He's really gettin' in the car without me!!

I ooo I ooo
I love you dad!

November 19, 2017

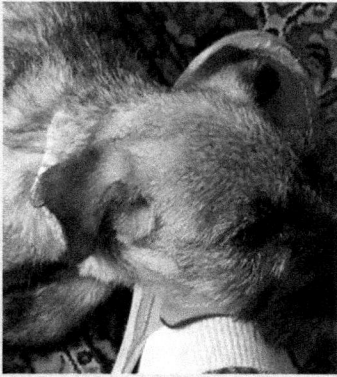

Charley here! It was a very uneventful and peaceful Sunday around here. Dad let me watch something called the 'GOAT' with him. Dad seemed happy but all I could think about was runnin' around that grass with all those people. Dad told me about grass. We don't have any of that kind of grass on Plum Island.

Mom and dad love to take 'cute' pictures of me but they don't really get me as my most exciting self. Here are two. One shows me and mom snuggling (which I love)! In the other one, mom caught me asleep on dad's shoe.

November 20, 2017

"Dad asked me to please try to stay still for a minute so he could take a picture for paws-terity, whatever that is.
So, here I am."

November 21, 2017

Charley again: Dad has been runnin' me ragged! I think he forgets I'm not even 3 months old yet. We have been workin' on a thing he calls 'fetch'. I call it controlled ice skatin' with a ball! He found this oversized tennis ball (THANKS PETSMART), that I can't fit in my mouth. Good thing I have puppy teeth. They are like sharp velcro! Then he wants me to 'drop it'! Hello! I can't even let go of it! Anyway, enjoy! I have to go and study. I hear there will be a test on 'come' and 'sit' later!

A note from dad:
Standard Schnauzers are commonly described as 'The dog with the human brain'.

November 23, 2017

Hi! First of all, Happy Thanksgiving (whatever that is) to all of my friends! This is my first Thanksgiving! It seems like everything, the sunrise, a warm lap, blowing leaves and hugs from mom & dad are all firsts. I bet you all remember when you were sooo excited to see, or smell, or do something for the first time!

I decided to give mom and dad a present for Thanksgiving (Is it OK to give presents on Thanksgiving?).

Anyway, some of dad's friends said I was too young for this stuff (I'll be 12 weeks tomorrow!!!) but dad insists I am a smart little girl and I can do anything that doesn't require opposing thumbs, whatever they are. Here it is!

On Facebook, there is a video showin' me doin' the 'sit - stay - come' thing.

November 26, 2017

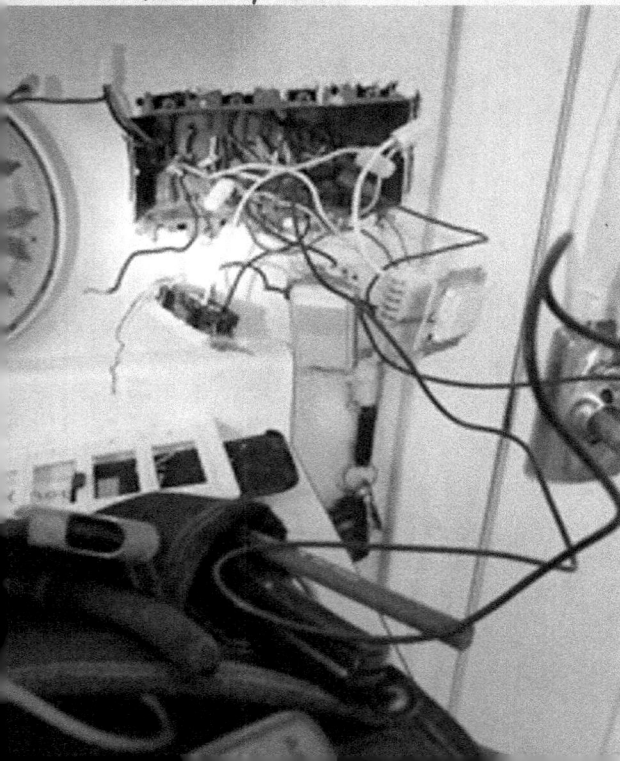

Charley, again! Thanksgiving was awesome! I got to meet my cousins from New Hampshire for the first time. They are Eliza, Emma and Augie. They tell me Augie is a 3-year-old Westie. I'm not sure what that is. Am I an Eastie? We ran and tumbled so much that dad and I left early 'cause he said he needed a 'time-out'! There were lots more extended family there but, enough about them.

Dad says I'm 3 months old now so I got him to take some pictures. He says I have fans and they are almost all gals. Cool! I am starting to learn about 'girl power'! For instance, I may have happened to get a tissue from the trash-can stuck in my mouth. Well, dad didn't like that one bit. But then I ran over to mom and got her to pick me up and dad was a lot calmer! Mom said it was girl power, heh, heh! Good to know!

"Yeah, I woke up the other day and dad was GONE!!! So I've figured out how to keep him in toe. Ha, ha! Get it?"

November 26, 2017

It's Charley again. Dad has been really busy with shoppin' and he had to put in a 3-way 'Smart Switch'! I heard him say a couple of new words but I'm not sure what they meant. He told mom he wished he was as smart as the d**n switch! I got mom to take a picture of the work-in-progress. I like that 'cause dad says that's what I am! I think he is happy because now he says, "Hey, Google, turn on the outside lights", and they come on all by themselves! Dad thought it was gonna be easy. Then he found out it wasn't wired like a regular 3-way switch.

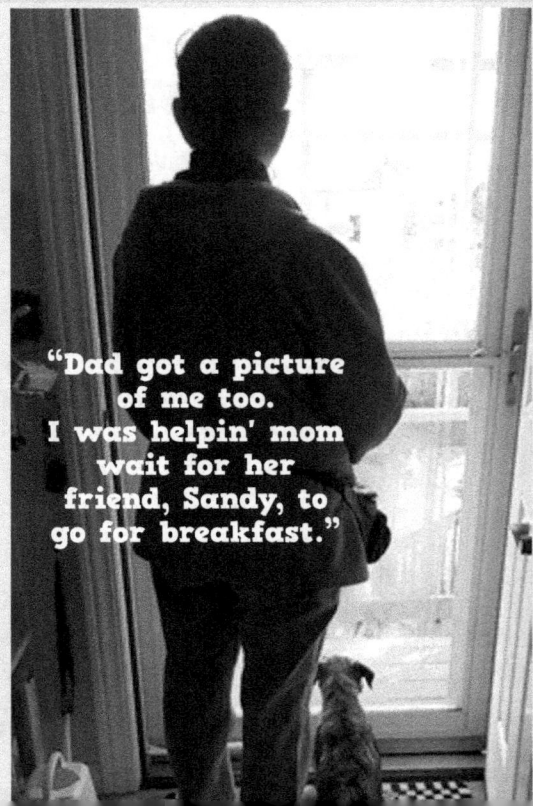

"Dad got a picture of me too. I was helpin' mom wait for her friend, Sandy, to go for breakfast."

CHAPTER 3
December 3, 2017

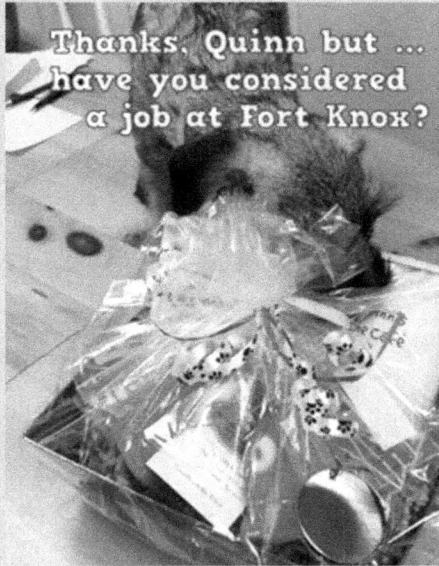

Me, when I was 6 weeks!

Charley here! I know, it has been a couple of days, but, it's not easy bein' a growin' pup! It's like doin' puberty in 3 weeks! Don't even get me started on the RULES around here! I mean, I love mom 'n dad but, for a while there, I thought my first name was 'No' and my last name was 'Dropit'! Yeah, I know I am Charley! Dad has been teachin' me about sarcasm. At least now I am starting to hear a lot of 'GOOD DOG!' That makes my day! Here are some pics to prove I'm growin'!

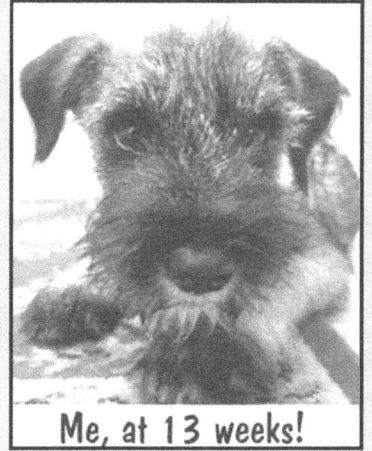

Me, at 13 weeks!

December 3, 2017

Thanks, Quinn but ... have you considered a job at Fort Knox?

Charley here! Yeah, I'm on a roll! I have to tell you about when I brought dad to the Tannery to pick up mom after a hard day of teachin' a thing called art. There were little humans there but I didn't see any other pups. Dad said I already have the art of "Unconditional Love", and I was better at it than a lot of humans! Hmmm?

Anyway, speakin' of love, there was a present waiting for me from Quinn, (from *Quinn's Canine Cafe*, here at the Tannery). Mom said it was a Christmas/Welcome to the Tannery gift. I don't know what a 'Christmas' is but I tore right into it anyway. There was a toy and treats and, well ... JACKPOT!!! Thanks, Quinn. I love you too!

This is gonna be very usefull in the next couple of months, mom. Let's go thank Quinn!

December 3, 2017

What? Me again! Dad says I'm gettin' to be a real motor-mouth, in more ways than one, whatever that means.

Anyway, dad & me were hangin' out in our new Key West room this mornin' and there was a picture of Tom (Yup, I had to learn about Tom Brady, even before 'sit'). Well I'm just restin' my eyes, if you know what I mean, and dad says, "Look, Charley, he's wearin' your shirt"! I looked up and saw Tom's shirt said 'PLIABILITY'. Yup, I've told you before that dad says I feel like a slinky! But ... I just couldn't hold my head up and told dad, "Don't wake me 'til kickoff at 1:00."

December 6, 2017

Charley here! I know a lot of you liked my pic on the front but I wasn't crazy about it and it was lookin' a little 'dog-eared'. After all, I am a big girl now! And I wanted to show off dad's artwork! That's my story and I'm stickin' to it!
Stand by, though, dad's gonna teach me to drive later!

Chuck & Charley

December 6, 2017

Charley here! Remember I told you that dad was gonna' teach me drivin'? Well, yesterday he did! He actually let me drive all by myself! But, I'm sorry, I don't think it's for me. There are these dog-gone RULES again! Dad says I have to look where I'm goin'. Yuk! When I'm on paw, I can run into anyone I want! I looked out the window once (there was a real hunk of a German Shepard in a white car) and dad was all ... HEY!, look where you're goin' and pay attention. I don't think so! He forgets my attention span hardly gets from me to the next treat at my age. Anyway, here is a photo!

On Facebook, there is a video showin' me drivin and tryin to reach the pedals.

December 7, 2017

Hey, Charley here! Hope you liked my video yesterday. Dad says I'm not even ready for a learner's permit. That's OK with me. I didn't like driving. Now ... riding and chewin' at that invisible thing that keeps hittin' my face ... well, I LOVE that part!

So, every time I see my girlfriends at the Artists Playground, they say how big I'm gettin'. Dad says he doesn't notice it as much, that is until he took this picture. He says I used to fit in one of the little rectangles! I'll be 14 weeks old tomorrow!

December 7, 2017

Hey, Charley here! Boy, was today exciting! Dad said he had a surprise for me and he sure did! When he opened the door downstairs it was all white outside! I don't know where he got all that cool white stuff but it was even comin' from up above somewhere. I think he hired an airplane or somethin'. Boy, was it fun!!! 'Course I'm no Kodi or invisible like Augie or snow magnet like Riley seems to be or a cool snow pro like Meta or even an expert like River but you watch, I'm gonna learn a lot this year!

December 13, 2017

So, it's Charley here, I think! This has been a very traumatic day for me. Actually, things were goin' pretty good, I thought. Mom & dad seem to be learning my routines pretty good. What can I say, I'm a natural teacher! But then dad says, right outta the blue, "come on Charley, let's get some of that scraggly hair off of you". So we go downstairs and dad puts me on a table and starts the machine. It's a little unnerving but he turned it on before a couple times and let me smell it so I wasn't too concerned. So, he runs it down my back (it felt good, actually) but then I heard him, "OMG!!!", he yells. "Who are you and what have you done with Charley?" It wasn't 'til I got upstairs to the mirror that I saw. OMG!!! I yelled. I look like a Schnauzer with a Westie body! Dad says it will be OK, and I really trust dad, but I tell you it won't be easy sleepin' tonight!

Before **After**

December 14, 2017

Charley again! Well, dad sure has been busy today. He talked with mom and they aren't gonna put up somethin' called a tree. I heard my name mentioned but I think they just don't want to overload my senses. So dad was all excited doin' the decoratin'. But then he got real serious when he was settin' up the little humans on the table ... and there are little tiny animals there too. Then he picked me up and explained about God. He tried to make a joke about God bein' dog spelled backward and I smiled. I mean, omg, I heard that one back in the litter!

Then he said he wished I could feel the peace that he and mom do because of bein' one in spirit. Well, dad, it's hard for me to tell you but we have a very strong spirit connection with each other and an especially strong one with our humans! And, you and mom and I haven't been together very long but I knew we were spirit buddies the moment we looked in each other's eyes. Oh, boy, I better show the pic 'cause I'm tearin' up.

December 15, 2017

So dad had one last decoration to hang. He hung it on the wall, at the top of the stairs, where everyone would have to see it. After I watched him hang it he brought me inside to the cozy room and had me sit in front of him on the floor. It was with his most serious voice that he told me about it.

Charley, he said, I made that sign with my own two hands and a lot of love. I want you to remember that no matter what goes wrong in our lives, whether it is an itch you can't reach or a beautiful love that is lost, God always wants us to see and feel the big picture! That picture is one of joy that is waiting for us as long as we listen to our spirit and try to live accordingly.

Then, he tossed me on my back and nuzzled my belly and we both laughed 'til we could hardly breathe.

December 20, 2017

Clysdale Charley here! So ... dad comes up to me yesterday, all smiles, mind you, and says, "Charley, you have a choice (first time this happened) between 2 Christmas presents, reindeer antlers or nice, shiny bells"! Well, I'm no Rudolf. so I grabbed the bells. Then, with a move I didn't know he was capable of, he had them around my neck! OMG! Now I sound like one of the horses in my original country of Germany, like I should be pullin' a sleigh or somethin'!

How am I gonna help Linda's Louie now? I was gonna 'neak up on those coyotes and scare 'em while Louie done 'em in! The way I sound, I couldn't 'neak up on Yankee Homecoming! Sorry, Louie! We haven't even met yet and I'm a disappointment to you. I'll try to figure somethin' out.

December 23, 2017

Charley again! Yesterday was my 4 months (a third of a year!) anniversary! Now, I can think of lots of little gifts they could have given me. For instance, a nice little piece of maple, or, I really like those hanging potholders, or, even better, remove the restrictions on those tasty, used tissues. I mean, your throwin' 'em out anyway! But, for the love of God, have you ever heard, "give the gift of WATER"? Well, that's what I got! Mom calls it a bath but it is definitely a shower! Mom says I have a thing called 'odor'. Of course, I'm a puppy! There's no dirt! How could anyone get that dirty in 4 months?

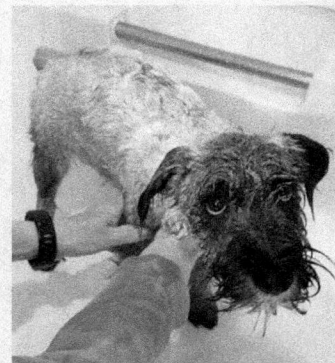

Anyway, it started out pretty good – that nice, warm water flowin' down my back, but then, OMG, all of a sudden it was like I was a fish! I thought I was gonna drown! But then it was over and I got all toweled off and even a treat cause I was a 'good dog'. Dad (of course) snapped a pic.

December 28, 2017

Charley here! Hope you all had a Merry Christmas! I know I did, but I'm not too sure about dad. He got a lot of ... well, let's say, Schnauzer related stuff. Mom did give him a smart bulb but even that is mostly so he doesn't step on me at night. It's pretty cool. He just says from bed, hey google, turn on the light, and there it is. He can even make it red or blue or whatever. Then he can get back into bed before he shuts it off. It's way over my head! He had me at the 'spill-proof bowl'.

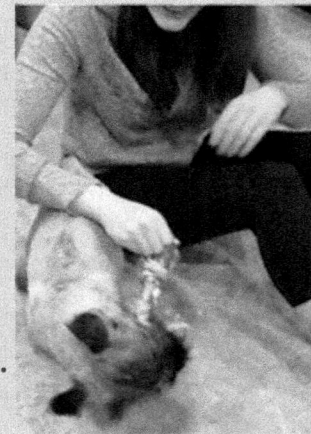

Anyway, he took pics but here is my fave - me and my cousin Kate!

Standard Schnauzers are not big Mini Schnauzers, nor are they little Giant Schnauzers. The three breeds are recognized as individual breeds by the American Kennel Club. The Standard Schnauzer is the original breed developed in Germany for farm work.

December 28, 2017

Charley here! So, dad's been givin' me these funny looks when I'm sayin' hi to my Facebook pals. I told him he should get his own account and he says this IS his account! I don't think so!

Just to show you what I'm up against, this is a pic of my Christmas stocking. Notice dad's stocking to the right. I could put 5 of mine into his! And, you could wait till the cows come home for him to open all his stockin' stuff! But then, the cows did come home, thanks to Auntie Cheryl Follansbee. She sent me a bull that couldn't even fit into my stocking! Everyone knows not to let your little furry animals near a Standard Schnauzer. But this was a furry BULL! Maybe she is tryin' to toughen me up!

Another chapter in my life is gone!

CHAPTER 4

January 1, 2018

Charlie here, & I'm back to normal! So, here's the story. I was jokin' (jokin', mind you) with dad when we wuz playin' out in the snow. Well, I looked at him and the way the sun wuz hittin' his head and I said, "Hey dad, you look like a cartoon"! Well, all he mumbled wuz somethin' like, "a cartoon, eh? Well, we'll see about that"!

So, now I have learned another thing along with sit, down, drop it & stop tryin' to sniff the toilet while dad is usin' it. It's – dad doesn't get mad but he sure gets EVEN! Here is what I mean. Oh, & dad says to make sure your sound is workin'.

So sorry! Once again, I just can't figure out how to put a video here!

January 10, 2018

Hey, Charley again! I sure miss gettin' in touch with all my friends but lately, it's just been the same old, same old around here. But dad told me that he met a handsome Boxer named Bently and he thinks he would like to play with me. He is only 9 weeks old but I think I kinda like younger men, if you know what I mean, girls! I mean, young enough to be fun, strong and interesting but not so young that I have to raise 'em. Bently's dad, Roland, said we could make a play date.

Anyway, I think that's why dad gave me a haircut today. He said it is close to my first 'real' puppy cut!

Personally, I like it, dad, but you coulda coughed up a little for a bow!

Charley

January 11, 2018

Charley here. Hey, is there a good K-9 attorney out there? I'm bein' set up. Yeah, their pinnin' a bum rap on me! OK, I'll admit, I never liked that little beady-eyed ferret anyway but, not enough to do him in!

I just happened to be prancin' past the kitchen and there he was, just lyin' there, not makin' a squeak! Then someone called the authorities (I think the UPSCA) and they're callin' me in for questionin'. They are callin' me an interestin' party. Well, I kinda like that! Oh, oh! I gotta go now. I'll keep you posted. Send treats!

Honest, officer, he wuz gone when (squeeeak) I entered (squeak) the room!

January 12, 2018

Yesterday, I caught a lot of flack for not destroying the evidence (of someone else's crime). Hmmm? I wonder why they are so knowledgeable about destroyin' evidence? Anyway, I only ate part of it, but I made sure no one will ever find the leftovers!

January 20, 2018

Charley here: Well I reached my 5 month anniversary yesterday but dad didn't get my picture. Mom was not feelin' good for a couple days and I guess it's dad's turn now. I think he is a lot better 'cause he said this morning he was feelin' like a dog! Wow! How good can it get?

As you know, dad's birthday was 4 days ago. Mom planned a private party for just the 2 of them but it didn't work out so good. See picture! But dad said I gave him the best present ... I told him that he would be 511 in dog years!

January 24, 2018

Charley here: Well, mom & dad are finally gettin' over their colds. It's about time if you ask me! I mean, how is it a person doesn't feel like playin' but takes time for trainin'? All work and no play is makin' Charley a dull girl!

Then, dad looks at me yesterday and says he'll be glad when my whiskers get longer 'cause I am lookin' disheveled! Hey, girlfriends, help me out here! I mean, how would you like it if your significant other had a tug-o-war with you, then tossed you around on the floor while ticklin' yer belly and then looked at you and said, "Hey, baby, yer lookin' a little messed-up lately."

Anyway, it's not all bad. You remember that little incident with the ferret, well, turns out, I miss chewin' on the little guy. But I found a fox just lyin' in the chair the other day! I think it was one of dad's birthday presents but ... well, ...you know how it is.

I know it's your fox, dad! I'm just guarding it for you!

January 26, 2018

Hi, Charley again. Well, dad & I have gotten ourselves into a real pickle. Dad is thinkin' it would be real fun to kinda document my first year with him and mom. Then he says (now get this), maybe other family and friends would like a copy, you know, like a gift! Well, right away, my girl power crew says he can't even afford my royalty fee! So he says we should get some feedback from our Facebook friends and tell them it would be all my posts in a bound 5½ x 8½ inch book of about 40-50 pages. Dad gave me a sample of the cover. What do you think? **Note frome dad: Guess it's grown!**

Charley
The First Year

c.f. lutz

January 26, 2018

Hey, Charley! Dad ordered some extra special dog treats for the game Sunday!

Pit of Despair

Hi, Charley again! As I said last time, mom 'n dad seem back to their old selves (hmmm, pardon the expression), but dad has seemed a little off this week. Then mom told me about the Super Bowl! Mom said dad went through the same kind of behavior last year and he didn't snap out of it 'til the last few seconds of the game. Wow! I hope he is better this year. I saw Tom Brady on TV and dad said he is an animal like me ... a GOAT! I don't get it.

January 29, 2018

Charley here. I know, I'm sorry. Two in one day! But I just had to tell you how dad 'n me watch TV at night. He says we don't really see eye-to-eye on the shows we like. For instance, I like the things called commercials a lot, you know, the ones for dog food. Some have real wolves in them and before I knew about TV I ran over with my hair up and growled and gave them my deepest puppy bark to protect mom and dad and they disappeared! Boy, was I proud I scared them away! Now I know the truth. Guess I'm funny, huh? But, guess what … mom 'n dad never made fun of me!

So dad & I sit and watch. He likes documentary stuff and I watch just to be with him. Sometimes there is somethin' funny and we both laugh. Of course, I don't do it out loud. It's more like when he tickles me! And sometimes we are sad, like when they show the dogs that are homeless or mistreated. That makes me real sad and when I look at dad, he turns away, like he is lookin' for somethin'.

C'mon dad, you promised! Animal Planet!

January 30, 2018

Charley again! So dad is always tryin' for just one more good picture of me. He keeps sayin' he wants me to show my 'happy' look. I keep tellin' him that I don't have a happy look that is any different than my normal 'look'! Let's face it (get it?), I don't have those muscles that make your lips curve up in a silly grin … nor would I want them! I would probably look like Dumbo with a moustache!

Anyway, dad tried and I tried and this is what we got!

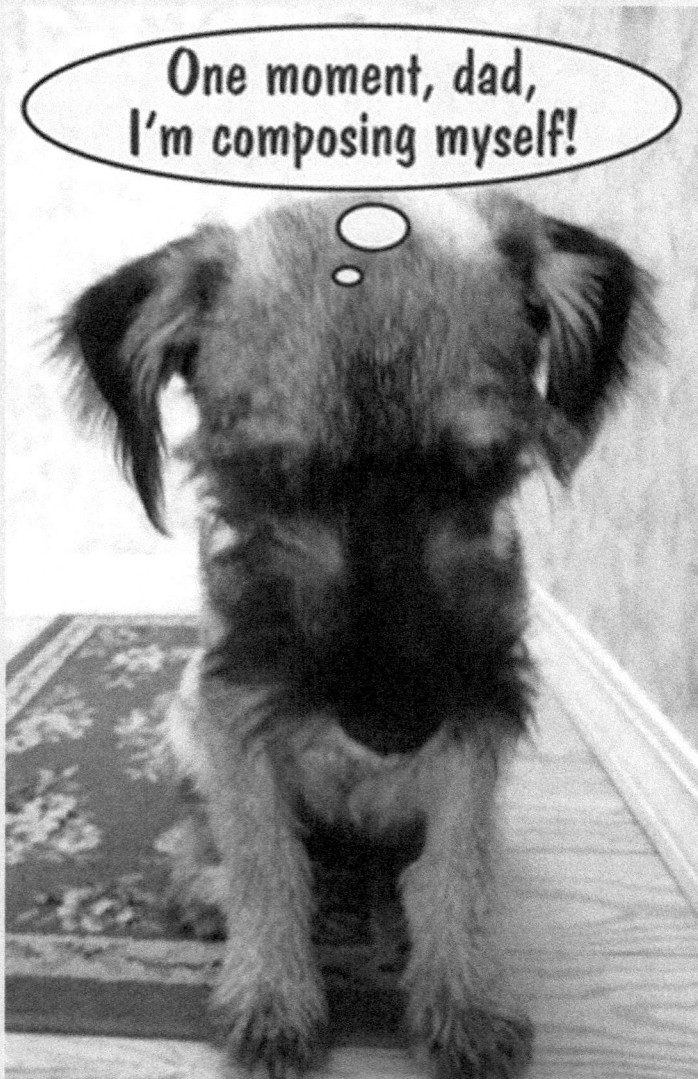

One moment, dad, I'm composing myself!

Huh? I'm ecstatic!

C'mon, Charley, show me your happy look!

January 31, 2018

Dad is the one with the mustache!

AAUGH!

not dad

Charlie again: Well, like I was sayin', dad & I love to watch TV together. Dad took a picture of me waitin' for the replay. No, not football. Dad rewinds the dog food commercials for me so I can see them again. The other pic is a selfie I tried to take (or is it an 'us-ie'?), but it's not so good. Hey, you try it not usin' yer thumbs! And that room they call the media room, like it was fancy or somethin'. But mom says dad built it all himself! Yup, the walls, the shelves & cabinets, the floor, everthin'!

And now there is a very comfy bed for me, but I like sittin' with dad. He holds me with his big, strong hands and I feel really safe. And ... guess what? I can jump up to his recliner all by myself now!

CHAPTER 5

February 2, 2018

Hey, Charley here. I'm pretty pooped (pardon the expression), this morning 'cause I had another rough, exhaustin' night at Puppy Kindergarten, down at Fit 'n Trim in Rowley. This was our 4th week and 2 to go. I haven't mentioned it before 'cause it's just goin' through the paces for me. Did you know that besides being referred to as the 'dog with the human brain', we are called 'kinderwachters' in Germany! Yeah, we protect children like nobody's business!

Anyway, my instructor, Kim, and her helper, Mary, are great. It's just takin' mom 'n dad a while to get it, especially dad. Mom says it's because he thinks he is a 'know-it-all', whatever that is. Here's a pic from last night's class. I call it the 'scratch-n-sniff' exercise!

February 2, 2018

Hi everyone! Charley here. So, mom and I had some girl time for a little sit down and, what they referred to as 'the talk'. She said she noticed I was getting' pretty chummy with one of the boy puppies at class. She said I might be growin' a little too fast and she wanted to go over some 'ladylike' things with me. I'm sure she saw I was nervous so she held my paw all the time. Well, girls, it was really nothin' to speak of. The best part, actually, was when she told me about the little procedure I was going to have at the vets in a couple of months. Mom was all serious and sad lookin' but all I could think about was wow, all that fun and no consequences! Woo hoo!!!

Then she said, Charley, we need to speak a little about dad, too. Oh, brother, I can't handle that also in one post. I'll tell you about that next time!

February 3, 2018

Charley here and disappointed! So dad is all excited about the big game and, well, if dad is excited, then so am I! So here I am, tryin' to be proactive, you know, and I got suited up so we could get a little warm-up in before tomorrow!

Hey dad, I yelled, let's go! You better throw a few to me 'cause I've seen how you operate on those metal knees! You'll be lucky to stay in the pocket!

Well, then he hits me with it ... we aren't playin', Charley, he says with I'm sure a grin. We're watchin' the game on TV! Well, you coulda knocked me over with a Milkbone. Talk about wantin' to crawl under my bed and hide! But dad hoisted me up by my shoulder pads, flipped me on my back and before I knew it, he was makin' that weird sound on my belly and I couldn't stop laughin' forever!

What do ya mean, we're not actually playin'?

February 4, 2018

Charley here: So here is part 2 of mom's discussion with me, the part about dad. I told mom that dad & I are together a lot but he still seems a little mysterious to me. Well, this is what she told me:

She told me that dad grew up in the Bronx, so he is always watchin' his back. Ah, that's why I can't 'neek up on him! Mom said when they were married 40 years ago that dad couldn't believe she didn't lock the door on Plum Island! Also, she says dad is hot! No, ladies, not THAT way. His body temperature! Mom is always cold. She says dad tells everyone that they were together for 5 years before he knew what her feet looked like! But then mom got serious and said she still hasn't figured him out! Here are the strange, but true facts, Charley. Your dad is multi-aptitudinal. He is as comfortable writing a poem as building kitchen cabinets. That's why he hasn't decided what he will be when he grows up. Yes, Charley, your dad is 73 years old, going on 14! He has B- blood, 2% of the population, (so some say he could be alien). For me, Charley, the jury is still out. But I'll tell you one thing for sure, Charley, dad says his definition of love is 'wanting to do for the good of another'. No one could love you and me more than dad does!

So that's it, folks. I'm gonna go find dad and lick him so much he'll hardly be able to breathe!

Whoa! Is that the best or what?

Yes, Charley, your dad is 73 years going on 14!

Dad could be an alien, Charley!

Mom, isn't alien just another way of sayin' "out of this world"?

February 9, 2018

Charley here! I see Pamela posted about Sheepdog training. Well, just want to let my friends know that I'm all over it!!!

Why, yes, I am a sheepdog in training!

February 14, 2018

Hey, Charley here. First of all, happy Valentine's Day to everyone! I love you all!

So, I asked dad to be my valentine. He said that although we love each other very much, mom is his main squeeze! But … he said I could be his 'K-9 Valentine'! I know, it has a nice ring to it, doesn't it? Dad got mom one of those LovePop cards with a teddy bear pop-up! Boy, did I want to chew, I mean, sniff that little bugger!

Then dad took me on his lap and told me somethin'. He said I have known about love since the day I was born, more than some humans learn by 70 or 80 years. He said I naturally knew about a thing called 'unconditional love' and that people didn't have to meet any of my expectations for me to love them! He said I don't care about anyone's philosophy or preferences or religion or how they look or nuthin'. He said I just go right for their spirit, like Cupid's arrow, and love them up! Wow, that really made me feel good!

I hope, as my Valentine's wish, all of you will love that beautiful spirit inside of you, first, and then share it with your favorite folks and, especially, your K-9 Valentines!

Dad's Valentines

February 16, 2018

Dr. Charley here! Yeah, I'm just kiddin', but I'm getting' there! I graduated from Puppy Kindergarten last night. Mom & dad seemed all proud and all but I just don't get it. I mean, I knew how to lay down when I was born! Why, we even ate layin' down! A few days later I learned to sit, all by myself. What's the big deal? Then, if I was stumblin' along and somethin' didn't look good I'd 'leave it' and, if I tried somethin' and it didn't taste good, believe me, I'd 'drop it'! Then there was the 'come' thing. Well, mom & dad know I love them and I always want to be with them … eventually!

CHARLEY

Fit-N-Trim
Dog Sport Training

PUPPY KINDERGARTEN GRADUATION CONGRATS!!

WOW! 6 weeks of schoolin'! That's, like, 25% Of my life! Can't we just hang out for a little while, dad?

Anyway, I did it! Now we can put that trainin' stuff behind us, or so I thought!

Today it was more of the walkin' on the leash thing with mom. Then practicin' come with dad and the new one 'roll over'! I thought I only did that when dad snores in bed! I mean, what's the point? I roll over and I'm a few inches from where I started and nothin' has changed! Talk about useless. It's terrible, I tell you. We might as well hang a 'Fit 'n Trim' sign over our front door!

Well, I might write tomorrow, that is if I can lift my little paws to the keyboard!

February 17, 2018

Dad says I can be his Sue Chef, but ... my name is Charley!

Hey, Charley here! So, I was 6 mos. yesterday or I'll be 6 mos. On March 1st, depending on how you count. I only care about 1 year 'cause my cousins Kody and Augie told me there could be a party and presents involved!

I love to help dad in the kitchen. Mom says 'cause he is 73 he drops more than he used to. That's a good thing. It drops & I'm on it! I have a confession to make. Sometimes when dad drops somethin', I yell (in my head) LEAVE IT!) & then I eat it! I feel like I'm in control!

Dad talks to me a lot when he is cookin'. Yesterday he was makin' French toast for him & mom and he asked me, Parlez-vous français? I thought, "Nein, dummkopf, I'm German!", but I didn't say it.

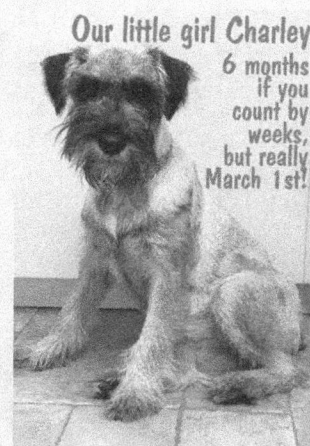

Our little girl Charley 6 months if you count by weeks, but really March 1st!

Later in the day dad made what he called his "Seafood in New Newburg Sauce", I think 'cause he uses coconut milk and gluten-free flour for mom. Dad said I am now his official Sous Chef and Taster. Well, I jumped all over that Taster job but I reminded dad my name is 'Charley', not Sue! Dad just kinda leaned on the counter and shook his head! Anyway, mom loved it and I felt very proud to have helped!

February 19, 2018

Hi everyone, Charley again. I asked dad to take a photo this morning so I could show you where we hang out while mom exercises. They call it the Key West room and dad built it last year before I was even born. I keep my present from Auntie Cheryl down there 'cause she lives in Florida, ha, ha, get it? I haven't met her yet but I love her 'cause the present smelled a little like chicken livers & popcorn, yummy.

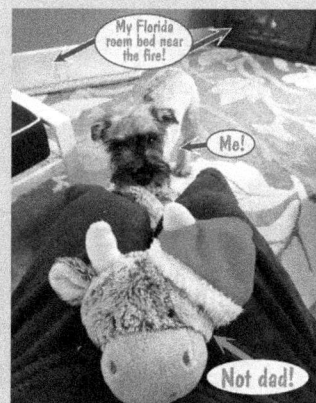

My Florida room bed near the fire!

Me!

Not dad!

So, every morning dad says, "Hey Google, turn on the heat." I don't know who he is speakin' to but mom thinks he may be alien! Anyway, we go downstairs, have breakfast and then to Key West. When we get there its all toasty warm and the fire is goin'! The door goes right out to our yard and dad says there will be a doggie door in the spring. I hope he remembers I don't have thumbs. Well, here is the picture. I wanted dad in it but his arm isn't long enough. The critter in front is Auntie Cheryl's toy, not dad. It has too much hair to be dad! Uh, oh, better go!

February 22, 2018

Charley here. Well, today I feel like I got the keys to the kingdom! Yup, mom 'n dad showed me the 'doggie' door(s)! Yup, there's more than one. I learned about 2 today and, I think I told you, there will be another in the 'Key West' room. First, they coated my paw with stuff and made me sign a non-disclosure form, but I refused to do it until they changed 'doggie' to 'Schnauzer' door. Humph! Doggie! No way!

Doggie Door! This is so humiliatin'! I'm not a silly 'doggie'. I'm a Schnauzer!

This was a big production, friends. I mean, the learnin' curve was shootin' right up there, if you know what I mean. First, there was the one from the house to the porch. That one was hard! No, not hard … hard plastic with magnets and everything. I can tell I'm gonna wanna go through there at low speed 'cause I could get a concussion!

Number 2 door goes from the porch to the actual outside! WOW! Did you hear that sound? Yup, it is the sweet sound of freedom! Anyway, I mastered them both and mom and dad were proud of me. Actually, I learned it after the first try … but they kept givin' me treats. Yup, I got dumb for a while!

WOW! They have more doors than "Lets-Make-A-Deal! At least this one is soft.

February 24, 2018

"Auntie Tina is watchin' my cousin Auggie and brought her for an impromptu play-date!"

Charley again! I had a great day today. First , I was doin' some leash trainin' with dad. We did OK but, between you 'n me, he's still got a ways to go.

Then, my Auntie Tina came over for lunch and, and, guess what! She is watchin' my cousin Auggie and brought her for an impromptu play-date! (Yeah, I know, but I learned that word from dad when I pooped in the wrong place once, but let's not go there.)

It was awesome seein' Auggie again. Seems like half my life has gone by since I saw her last! Oh, yeah, it really has. Anyway, it was great. We romped all over the house and the yard. I think Auggie was getting' a little irritated with me bein' such an exuberant host. All I can say is, "Get over it, Auggie! I'll be at your place next weekend!"

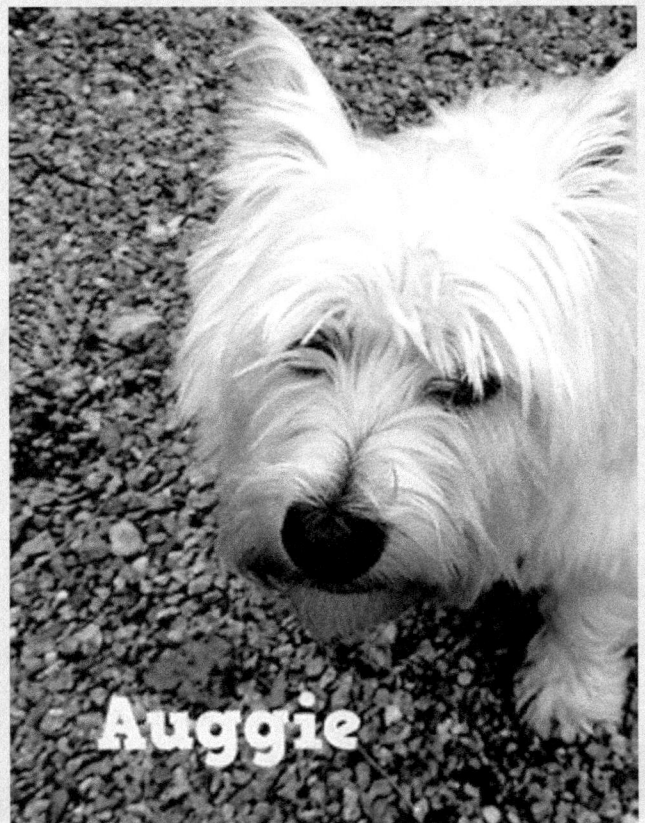

Auntie Pat! This Fountain of Youth really works!!!

Just lettin' her feel good!

Hey, Charley, help a girl out, would ya? Just whisper in my ear, what are they feedin' ya?

How long does he make you sit here for that puny treat?

It varies, Auggie. But I've found it best to let dad think he's in control!

Auggie

February 26, 2018

Charley here! So, I've been tryin' to get dad's attention all afternoon! He was workin' on that computer for the longest time. Me, I wanted some play time. Besides, I needed to get on the computer myself to write a post to my friends. BTW (dad told me what that means. Cousin Auggie said it means Big Tough Westie) but, BTW, dad says he thinks I have more friends than he does. Mom says to try to ignore him. Mom says to put his feelin' sorry for himself in the same category as his 'senior moments'. I asked dad what those 'senior moments' were and he said it is like goin' to the prom – much more important than 'junior moments'. I don't know, I think I saw mom smirkin' while he was tellin' me!

Anyway, I tried all my tricks. I dropped almost every toy at his feet! I barked when there wasn't anyone at the door. I even jumped up in his lap when he turned around for somethin' (yeah, I can do that now!), but, nothin' worked. Finally, after what seemed like years in puppy time, he showed me what he was workin' on. He said he just got new grocery bags and had to personalize them. He said it makes shoppin' more fun! The pics are below.

Then he grabbed all my toys, threw me on the bed, piled the toys on top of me and then started the ticklin! OMG!!! I laughed so hard I thought I was gonna pee in the people bed! And dad, dad said he couldn't take any more of me jumpin' on him 'cause his belly was hurtin' from laughin' so much! After we calmed down, dad looked at me and said, "Now that, young lady, was a senior moment!"

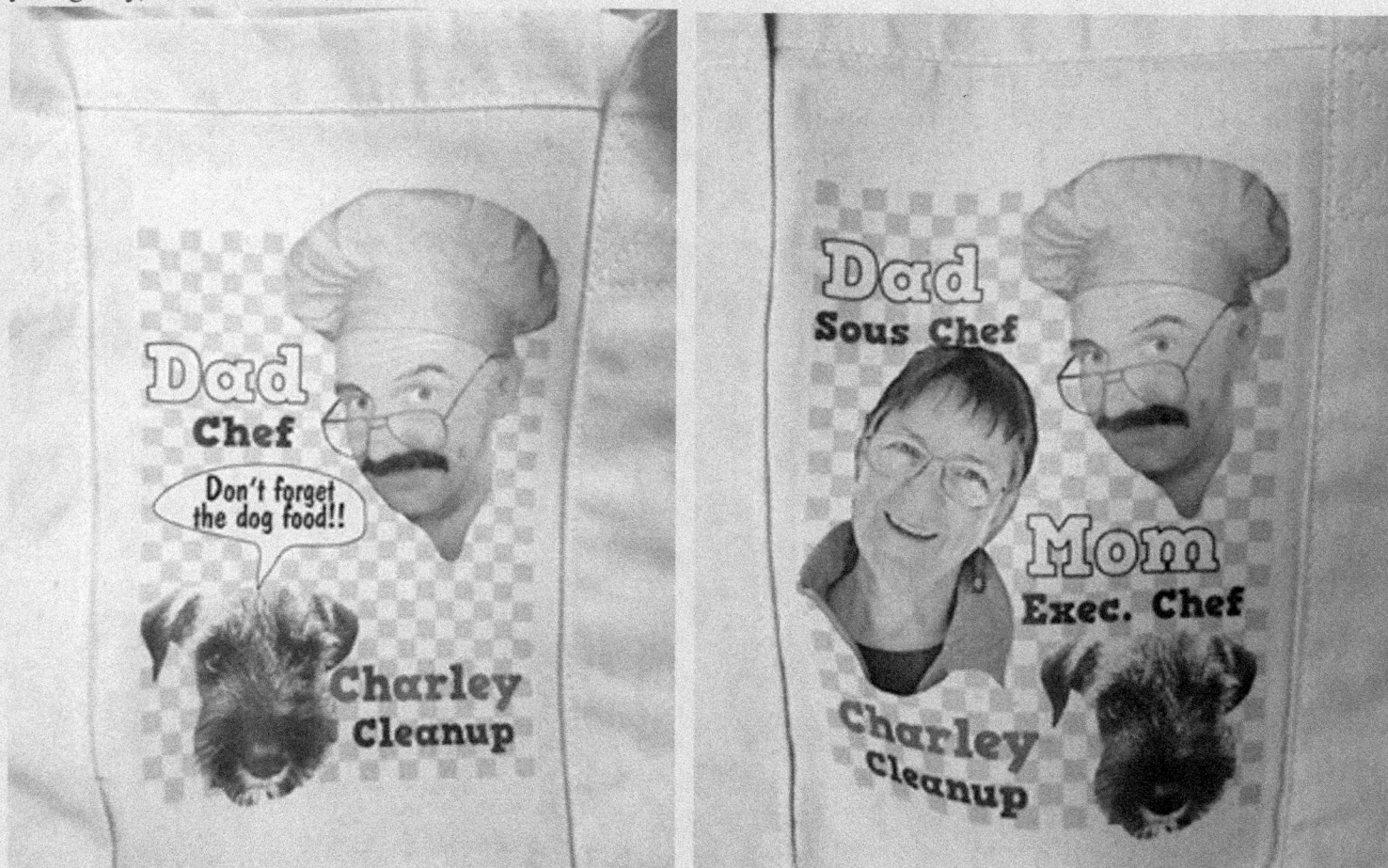

February 28, 2018

Charley here! Hey, I like dad's poems and all, but I coulda really taken care of that bunny in the yard! (Note from dad: Charley is referring to a poem I wrote in another post)

Anyway, I just had to tell you all that I have been blown away by a recent gift. So, I go to the studio, my usual self, you know, nonchalant yet ready to rock 'n roll at the drop of a hat! So mom says, "Hey, Charley, Tina left you a present." Well, Tina Kennedy gave me a present before and it was pretty cool. But, this was a little floppy thing that I hardly wanted to wrap my fairly new choppers around. Well, mom brought it home and I noticed it under the table. Well, I thought, it is a gift, so I'll give it a little chew and a toss! OMG, I don't know what it is about that little goofy thing but I have hardly been able to put it down long enough to eat or ... well, you know! Thanks, Tina! I love you!

CHAPTER 6
March 4, 2018

Hey, Charley here again. What a weekend this has been friends! I turned 6 mos. Old on March 1st. and boy did it hit the fan ever since! On Friday, me 'n dad had to go up to The Artists Playground to set up the tables for the Tannery Arts Camp sign-ups at 8 a.m. Saturday morning. Dad said he wasn't sure if he would be able to get up town with the floodin'. but, he made it after all and he told me that by 6:30 a.m. there were already folks waitin' to sign kids up. Then dad had to go get mom for the 10 o'clock art class and come home and get me and get back up-town before they closed the turnpike. Whew! Then … Tina wuz bringin' cousin Auggie after the class so Auggie could ride with me to go home to Durham, NH. DOUBLE Whew!! Anyway, it all worked out.

The highlight was that my cousins Christopher and Trisha and my 2nd cousins Emma and Eliza gave dad a mug they got in New York with MY picture on it. I am eatin' a taxi cab! I don't get it! Maybe I thought it was fare game! Get it? FARE game! They also gave mom some earrings she loves but I don't think I'll ever get to wear 'em.

Personally, I think it's the spittin' image of me!

So, as I said, we had a GREAT time with Trisha, Chris, Emma and Eliza. I couldn't get over how good Eliza & Emma were ridin' Eliza's new electric scooter! Dad told me he had to make his own scooter out of a wooden crate, a 2x4, a couple of sticks for handles and a roller skate, when he lived in the Bronx.

March 4, 2018

Dad took a 6 month pic and, even though I don't look like a 'cover dog', I was with mom and those are my favorite ones!

March 5, 2018   "Sometimes the alibi is worse than the crime"!

Dad made me write that and he says I can't Facebook for 24 hours. It's all 'cause of a little, teenie-weenie incident with mom. When she overheard me 'splainin to dad that she was kinda old and might not remember it exactly how it happened and then, well, it wasn't pretty, friends!

Between you 'n me, I think he just wants to use the computer himse ... uh, oh! Here he comes ...

March 7, 2018

Charley again. Well, things have smoothed right out around here now that I can jump up to dad's lap and love him up. So last night dad asked me if I wanted to go with him to the studio to get mom or if I wanted to practice my guarding duties. I decided to practice 'cause if no bad guys get in the house I get a treat! It's pretty easy work but I ain't gonna tell mom 'n dad.

> Yes, we're goin' upstairs. All of a sudden we feel surrounded by paparazzi!

> I went right to my hangout to snuggle with "Twinkle Fancy Face".

Turns out, I should have gone 'cause girlfriend Tina Kennedy got me another present! I wish I coulda licked her all up and given her my patented Schnauzer Wiggle! She sent me a little Unicorn buddy who I knew right away would be a great snuggler. Dad helped me look up her (well, yes, she's a girl) name on the internet. Her name is "Twinkle Fancy Face". Thank you sooo much Tina!!!

March 13, 2018

Hey, friends, Charley again! So, I was feelin' a little down and confused. Dad, of course, reads me like a book and he asked what was wrong. I explained as best I could and he seemed to understand. Dad said that when he feels like I did, he sometimes writes about it Well, I love dad's poems, but I said I could never be a poet.

Well, dad said I don't have to be a 'poet' to write somethin' poetic. He said I just have to write from my heart more than my head and that I can't worry what folks think 'cause most of them have the same feelin's but might have trouble expressin' them! Do you see why I love mom 'n dad so much? Well, here goes!

Dad's Gone! by Charley Lutz

One minute ago I was happy and sure
But that chew toy has now lost it's allure.
'Cause now I'm feelin' a little bit sad.
Why do you have to do this, dad?

I knew it was comin' when you put on your hat
And you gave mom a kiss and me a pat.
You said lots of words that I don't know.
I only know drop-it, leave-it, come and no.

Then, before I knew it you went out the door
Leavein' me with that pat and wantin' more!
Mom seemed so happy, like she understood
And she gave me a pat, like it was all good!

You guys keep usin' those things called words
But to me it's only actin' like nerds.
You don't seem to get it but really you should
'Cause I worry sometimes that you're gone for good.

I've learned over time that you always come back
But I worry 'cause judgein' time is somethin' I lack.
I've got the solution & know what we can do.
The answer is simple – I'll go everywhere with you!

March 15, 2018

Hi Friends! It's Charley again and I'm exhausted!

(I got that word from dad 'cause he came downstairs the other day and said he had a really tough night. Mom felt bad for him and asked what was wrong. Well, dad said he dreamt of mufflers all night and he was exhausted when he woke up! I didn't get it but mom threw a kitchen sponge at him.)

C'mon dad, give it up!!! You know Tina sent this Unicorn as a gift for ME!

Anyway, I told you about the great unicorn that Tina Kennedy got me. Her name is "Twinkle Fancy Face". Well, it turns out that dad has always liked unicorns! Who knew, right? He keeps tryin' to take ol' Twinkie and play with her. Then I try to get her back and we have a colossal tug-o-war!

Finally, mom said she had enough and had to step in. She said 'cause she was my gift I could play with her all day but at night, when I take Twinkie to bed, dad can hold onto her horn, gently! Whew! Ol' level-headed mom! Who knew that either? I'm tellin' ya, life is an education around here!

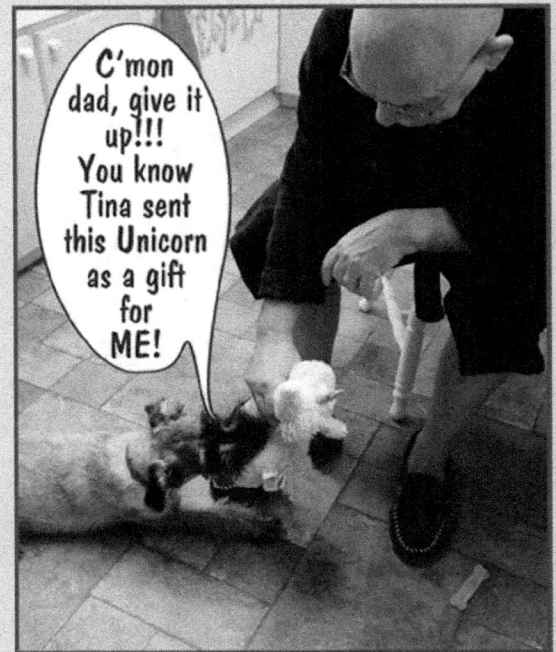

March 17, 2018

Hey, Charley here. Well, mom is always laughin' at the way I sleep with my head on (or in) dad's slippers. She thinks it's 'cause I don't want him 'neakin' off without me. Well this picture proves I have outgrown that silly little issue!

March 19, 2018

Charley here. Well, dad comes over to me today, all pleased with himself and grinnin' from ear to ear. "Charley", he says, "I've got some bling for you, and, congratulations! You are number 00108! I have your first little, golden dog license!"

OK, dad, let me try to get this straight. We got this license so YOU can keep me to live with you. So shouldn't YOU have to wear it?

"Oh, thanks, dad! Now when I sit on your lap I can drive the car too!"

So, dad explained that it wasn't that kind of license and that it was kinda a license to be a dog. But, I told him, I'm already a dog! If I didn't get the license, would I disappear? Well, he said no, that it was really a license that said him and mom could have me live with them.

I really thought hard as I could about this and told dad that I already had to wear one tinkling thing (it drives me nuts) that shows I got my shots. That's OK 'cause, well they are my shots and my butt I got 'em in. "But dad", I said, makin' myself as puffed up and serious as a 6-month-old can, "if it's so you can have me livin' with you 'n mom, shouldn't YOU wear it?" I think I won … for now!

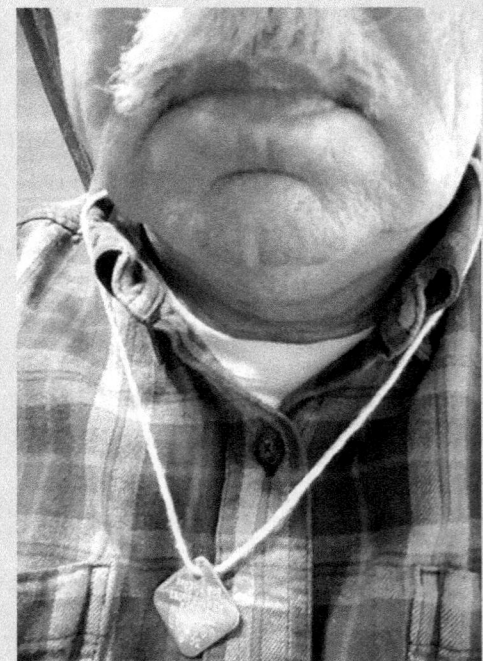

March 19, 2018

Hi everyone, Charley here. I know, I know, it's been a few days but things have been pretty hectic around here! Seems mom 'n dad got their Rav4 before I was born and, unbeknown to me, they haven't been crazy about it. They have tried their first (and last) lease. Guess they worry about damage and stuff. So, dad brought the car in for service and saw a Prius Prime, whatever that is, and they are tradin' for that. Dad even ordered a EV chargin' station 'cause it runs partly on 'lectricity! I haven't even been asked for an opinion yet but I'll let you know how I like it!

Meanwhile, the bright spot was that we got to go to Kodi's house for dinner yesterday! And, and … wait 'til you hear this! I been thinkin' Kodi was my cousin but it turns out he is really my nephew! It gets even BETTER! Turns out Erik is my brother!!! I didn't think there was much family resemblance, but dad says as Erik gets more gray hair … hmmmmm? Then dad says to picture Erik with a moustache. OMG!! We could be TWINS! That's all I can say for now. I'm gonna have to really chew on this news for a while!

CHAPTER 7

April 4, 2018

Charley here … barely!

Dad says I can only write a little 'cause I need to rest. I've been doin' that a lot since yesterday. I got spayed yesterday! I think they call it spay 'cause it sounds more fun than a hysterectomy plus! Anyway, mom and dad didn't tell me about it 'til we got to Newbury Animal Hospital. When they told me Dr. Grillo was doin' it I wasn't worried at all. He is my pal. I think dad was worried more than me. I heard mom say something about 'helicopter dad', whatever that means. Dad took a picture before I went and then another one last night. I don't remember last night. But, this morning, even though it was the first time I ever heard that THUNDER stuff, I ate my breakfast and dad gave me one of those nice pain pills. Hmmm, think it's time for another nap!

I don't remember much about last night except snugglin' a lot with dad. He sure makes me feel like everythin' is gravy 'n bully sticks! (It's a dog thing)

April 10, 2018

Hey, Charley here! Dad has been kinda 'under the weather' for a couple days. I was eavesdroppin' the other day and heard dad tell mom he was feelin' like a dog! Yippee!, I yelled. I'm winnin' this battle! But it turns out that for a human to feel like a dog isn't a good thing. So, I'm thinkin', the next time I'm 'off my game' I'll say … bummer, I feel like a human! Anyway, dad says I have to start earnin' my keep. He put up a sign that the neighbors gave us but he says the sign people don't have a clue what a Standard Schnauzer looks like. He says it looks like a Mini Schnauzer. He also got our EV Chargin' Station installed. So, after all that work, I'm helpin' him recuperate!

Quiet, mom! Dad said I could be the power in his 'Power-Nap'!

CAUTION
PROPERTY PROTECTED By STANDARD SCHNAUZER

April 12, 2018

Hey, girlfriends, Charley here and I am needin' some serious help from you gals. There aren't many 'doggie' mirrors around here but I finally got a gander of myself in the upstairs full-length mirror and … OMG! I mean, get a load of what a mess I am. I give a whole new meaning to 'dog-eared'! I get it. Mom and dad have been real busy but hey, I need some help!

Dad has been brushin' me, which I would gladly do myself except for that 'thumbs' thing. But I need serious help. Dad seems to be waitin' for me to be well healed from my little hyster , er surgery. Well, it's been 10 days and I am ready to go (if you know what I mean, girls, like, no 'mornin'-after' worries except for maybe a Milkbone hangover).

So, if you happen to see dad in your travels, try to nudge him in the Schnauzer make-over direction. He doesn't realize how we gals need our hair to look good. If you take a peek under that hat he always wears, you'll understand why! I'm just sayin'!

April 16, 2018

Hi everyone! Charley here!

So, to make a short story even shorter, dad was watchin' mom change her Masterson palette this mornin' and he said "Wow" and took a picture of it. Then he said, "Charley, I'm gonna use this to illustrate a little story I wrote and, bein' that it's a rainy, story-tellin' day, I'll read it to you right now". Here it is!

Jimmy "Passion Fruit" Koala loved his native land. More important, he loved the fish that occupied the coral reefs to the west of the island of Muku, a little known spot of land that is just a coconut throw from Hawaii. Of all the beautiful finned inhabitants of the reef, Jimmy loved a certain rainbow colored trigger fish the best. He saw this species for the very first time one evening as he paddled over the reef on his way home from a successful day of spear fishing. Suddenly, an object about the size of a barracuda appeared next to his boat. It was every color of the rainbow and stuck straight out of the water, with only its tail submerged to propel it along. The eyes, which were even with Jimmys', peered at him quizzically.

This was the most fantastic creature that Jimmy had ever seen. It was like a swimming artists' palette. The only thing he could think of was to somehow protect this oddity from those who might harm it. In an instant he knew what to do! He said, "I shall name this fish a Humuhumunukunukuapuaa, (pronounced humuhumunukunukuapuaa)." He knew that this would protect it because from then on anyone who saw the fish would say "look, there's a humuhumunukunuku…", and before they finished, it would safely swim away.

the Humuhumunukunukuapuaa

April 19, 2018

Hey, everyone, Charley here again. So mom & dad say they can't believe how long I am for 7½ months, especially when I do my trademark lay-down with my hind legs straight out! They laugh, but where do they expect me to put them, behind my ears? They say they don't think Lucy was as long at this age. I say "vive la différence"! (that's French that I heard on TV)

Well, the big news is that I learned a new trick. Dad says, "c'mon up, Charley", and I jump right up onto his lap. Mom 'n dad are jealous 'cause I can jump so effortlessly!

(I like doin' what dad says but he doesn't know that I like seein' out the window when I'm up there)

The best thing is that now I do it without even bein' asked! Yup, I sometimes get a runnin' start from the other room and really jump on dad! I think he really likes it when I almost make his chair go over backward when he is havin' his mornin' coffee.

BTW, does anyone out there know what the word 'damn' means, especially when said with much exuberance?

April 19, 2018

Hi friends! It's Charley again.

So, yesterday I had a rather lengthy sit-down, er, I guess, lay-down talk with dad. I told him that I was feelin' a bit overwhelmed & underappreciated lately, what with all this learnin' about how to fit in as a family Schnauzer. Well, dad said, I know it's a lot to take in your first year, what with house breakin' leash walkin', birds zippin' overhead and things bloomin' that you have never seen before. That's why I have a special treat to show you. Then he takes me into where we watch the moving things (I think they call it the medium room). He said, "Charley, sometimes you want to see closer, especially when there are puppy-dogs there" and with that, he lifts up my front feet to this thing and low 'n behold, it made it easier to watch the movin' things! Thanks, dad! This is awesome!

Psssst! Friends! I didn't want to spoil dad's fun but I heard him talkin' to mom about when Lucy was here and every time he turned on that thing the Animal Channel was on. So when he built the entertainment center he added the bar to keep her away from the controls & it also helped us watch the Animal Channel! I'm just sayin'!

Charley Bar

April 23, 2018

Hi friends! Charley here. So, dad saw my comment after our talk the other day … you know, when I said he really built that TV bar for Lucy. Yeah, I forgot that dad can read my posts too! (Dad reminded me not to write anything in here I wouldn't want the whole world to see) Anyway, he said he was gonna build somethin' just for me. Sure enough, yesterday he brought this thing up from his shop, a toy box just for me, with my name on it and everythin'! Turns out it is not quite done 'cause dad wanted my and, of course, mom's input. Now he has some fillin' & sandin' to do & he is gonna stain the letters so they stand out. I'll post a pic when he's done.

OMG, friends, don't I have the best mom 'n dad in the whole world!!! You shoulda seen my wiggle-butt go!!!

OMG! Fox! Get your head down or she'll find us again!

CHARLEYS TOYS

At first I thought it said "Charleys Boys"!

I hope dad doesn't expect me to put this stuff back!

April 25, 2018

Hi friends! Charley here! 'Member I said I would show you my new toy box after dad did the finishing touches? Well, here it is. I think mom is trainin' dad to put my toys in it before we go to bed!

Thanks, dad! Now it will be easier for you to put my toys away!

CHARLEYS TOYS

April 26, 2018

Hey friends, Charley again! I know, you're probably sayin' Oh, no, not her again! But dad's been on a roll lately and I can't wait to tell you about what he is doin'.

So, remember I told you I was feelin' a little frumpy and need a little makeover? Well, dad got right on it. Seems like he used to have a bigger shop but it got downsized to make what they call the 'Key West' room in the basement. I heard him tell mom that Schnauzers (that's me) don't like havin' their back to the door where someone could 'neak up on 'em. Well, yeah! After all, I'm the protector around here.

So here is what dad came up with. He put me in one of the pics and I wasn't happy, not bein' prettied up yet. Dad said he doesn't need a grooming arm 'cause he's been doin' a little here and there and I'm used to standin' still. Hmmm, we'll see! I don't do much standin' still … I'm just sayin'!

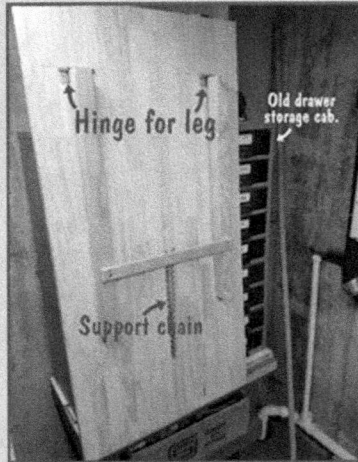

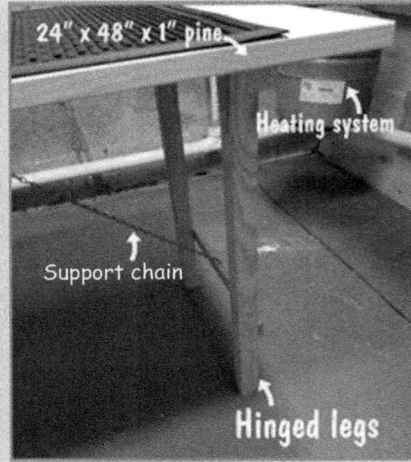

April 26, 2018

Charley here. OMG! Did I find the perfect place for a nice little siesta! Unfortunately, mom didn't share my enthusiasm. How was I to know that down comforter was so important.

But, I explained to mom that I was only half enjoyin' the bed 'cause I am guardin' Louise's house too. We have to look out for our friends, don't we mom?

Dad is teachin' me to think fast!

April 27, 2018

So, Charley here. I just can't understand it! I have great things to chew (like the bully stick in the picture), but for some crazy reason I like to be able to touch dad's foot or shoe while I'm chewin' my bone. I even like to lay my head on his shoe when I'm sleepin'. Dad says that if I know he or mom are around I feel safe.

So, now I'm wonderin' … WHO'S PROTECTIN' WHO??

April 28, 2018

Charley here friends!

So, dad was readin' to me (yeah, he does that sometimes), about how pets look like their owners. Well, I have no problem with that concept but dad kinda laughed it off. Dad insisted it was hogwash and he said, "Charley, I'm tapin' this stylus to your paw and you draw what dad looks like to you". After a few minutes we looked at the results. OMG!!! We were both floored … especially when we held our pics up next to each other! CAN YOU SAY TWINS?

I know, friends, I don't know what to say either. Here we are and, don't worry. I asked dad to add names so you would know who was who.

A History of the Standard Schnauzer
from / by The American Kennel Club

The Standard is the original Schnauzer, progenitor of the Miniature and the Giant. In Germany, the Standard Schnauzer is known as the Mittelschnauzer ("medium Schnauzer").

During the long centuries before mechanized agriculture, the world's farmers strove to breed versatile dogs to use as all-purpose helpers. The farmers of different regions found diverse solutions to the same challenge, resulting in such varied breeds as the Kerry Blue Terrier (Ireland), Rat Terrier (United States), and Belgian Tervuren. Germany's entry in the quest for an ideal farm dog was the breed that would come to be known as the Schnauzer.

A creation of the Middle Ages, the breed came of age in the verdant farm country of Bavaria. Like the world's other barn-and-stable breeds, multitasking Schnauzers made their bones as ratters, herders, guardians, and hunters. Standards bear a superficial resemblance to several terrier breeds of Britain, but the breed is a product of Continental herders and working dogs.

During the birth of Europe's organized show scene in the 1870s, the "Wire-haired Pinscher" proved to be a dashing show dog. By the turn of the century, fanciers began exhibiting the breed as the Schnauzer ("whiskered snout"). Schnauzers were in America since at least 1900, but it took until the '20s before they clicked with pet owners. In 1933, the Schnauzer's AKC parent club divided into separate clubs for the Standard and Miniature breeds.

CHAPTER 8
May 2, 2018

So, I turned 8 months old yesterday and dad gave me a bath and a bit of a haircut. I heard him talking to mom and they said they want to do just a little at a time so I would adapt to it. I don't think they realize just how adaptable I am!

May 2, 2018

Charley again, friends.

You know, I think I am losin' it! Every mornin' I wake up I go through my 'big girl litany' of things to remember for the day like:

• don't yank on anythin' that is attached to a human,

• don't chew anythin' colorful that is attached to the ground,
(why do they make them flower things so yummy lookin' anyway?)

• don't feign affection for dad by lickin' his mustache after he eats, etc., etc.

Believe me, friends, there are many more verses to this litany! But, what bugs me most is when I tell myself I will NOT sleep on dad's slippers. After all, I'm 8 months old and a big girl now and I have a very comfortable bed. I thought I was doin' so good & then, this morning, dad left this picture next to my breakfast bowl. I mean, I could be wrong, but I think he likes that I forget.

May 3, 2018

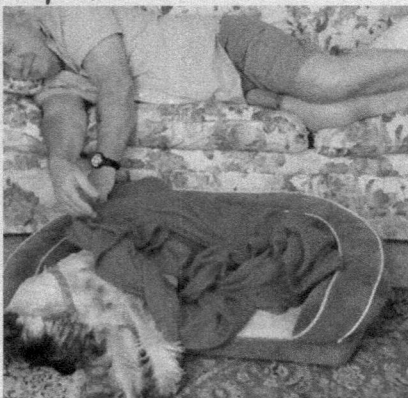

Charley here. The yard was great this morning on Plum Island! Mom has these things she calls daffodils, but I call them lollipops!
Then, after lunch, it started to rain so I taught dad my power-nap. Poor dad. He used to have a nice blankie but mom gave it to me!

May 8, 2018

Hey friends, Charley here. So, dad was all excited yesterday 'cause he said he got me a present. Well, I have been kinda askin' for some bling so I went into the whole, full monty, butt wag! Lo 'n behold, he pulls out this sorta pink thing and shows me my name and phone number on it. At first I thought he called it a nightingale collar and was sayin' I was a birdbrain but it is a Martingale collar. So dad fixed the size (it can barely go over my head) and I went into my act. Dad, (I made it sound like I couldn't breathe and coughed a couple times) I thought you were getting' me some bling?

He said, "Knock it off Charley. I'm wise to your tricks, and, maybe some bling when you are a year old"!

Wow, and you ladies thought you have it bad. Guess this isn't the time to ask about a cell phone.

May 11, 2018

Hi friends, it's Charley here! I am soooo psyched! Now that I'm 8 months old, I guess dad thinks I can help out around here. He told me he is givin' me the job title of 'FDGD in Training'. That means Front Door Guard Dog! I can hardly contain myself. Dad says if I do good on this assignment, the sky's the limit! Of course, I asked dad if I get a badge but he said no. Dad said I'll look so intimidatin' that no one would get close enough to see my badge! OK, I gotta go. I'm practicin' 'the look'.

Is this where you want me to guard dad?

Please don't be afraid, friends. Dad is trustin' me with this big 'sponsibility and I'm usin' my mean look to keep any intruders away!

FEAR THE BEARD

May 13, 2018

Hi friends, a very happy Charley here! So, yesterday there was a combo party for Kyle. He is actually my nephew but I don't think he realizes it. Kyle's birthday was Friday and he is leavin' for Air Force Basic Trainin' on Tuesday. There was a big party at Kyle's house but I couldn't go. Somethin' about too many people, kids and me bein' a puppy. Hello! I'm already doin' guard duty, ain't I? Anyway, I was bummed that I wouldn't get to say bye to Kyle or say Happy Birthday. Then, OMG, after mom 'n dad came home (I can stay home myself now), that tingely thing happened and mom spoke to someone and then, soon after my sister-in-law Tanya, my brother Erik and Kyle showed up. They made up an excuse of bringin' a Mother's Day present but I knew they really came to see me! Well, here are the pictures. I'm sure gonna miss you, Kyle!!!

May 17, 2018

Hi folks, it's Charley. Well, I have had an interesting couple of days. For one thing, I thought my dad could handle anything but I'm not sure about them guys upstairs. The other day we was wrestlin' as usual but this time I just about had him! No kiddin', I was goin' in for the kill, friends. Then, all of a sudden, there was a huge bang and I looked out the window, completely losin' my concentration.

For the love of God, dad, I yelled, what was that? He calmly said it was thunder 'n lightenin', lookin' upstairs. They kept makin' noise, even louder! Dad, why don't you get rid of them? He said they used to frighten Lucy and asked how come I wasn't afraid. Well, I'm a big girl Schnauzer and ain't afraid of nothin', I said. Well, dad seemed surprised, yet pleased that they didn't bother me but I haven't seen him make a move to get rid of them! I didn't even know there was anyone livin' up there. I'll have to figure out how to see them.

May 18, 2018

Hi friends, Charley here. Well. It wasn't pretty & might have lacked my usual finesse, but I rescued my first damsel in distress today. Yup, it was mom, and she called me 'her knight in rusty armor'!

You see, I was walkin' past the bath and thought I would get a little splash from mom, who was in the shower. I stuck my head in and there was mom in her squeaky-clean humanness but, outta the corner of my super observant eye, I spied a little black thing with twice as many legs as me! Well, I jumped right into that shower, with little regard for my own safety, and dispatched the thing with one lick! Mom said her little girl was quite impressive! I can't wait to find out what feats I'll perform when I am 9 months old!

Don't worry mom, I took care of that spider for you!

May 18, 2018

Hi friends! Obviously, it's Charley, cause dad's out of it! I really put him to the test yesterday! Anyway, it's a great Sunday for computin' and schnoozen. (That's a Schnauzerism for snoozin', ha ha!)

Quiet, mom! I just licked dad into unconsciousness!

May 21, 2018

Charley here! Just lettin' you know I' almost 9 months and on duty! But, don't worry if you are my Facebook friend, I won't hurt you!

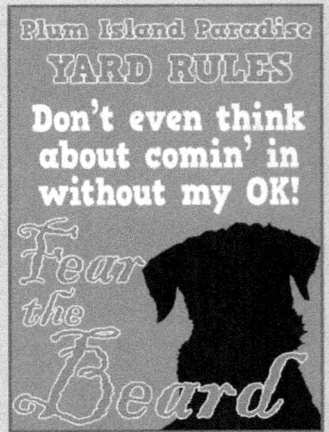

Plum Island Paradise
YARD RULES
Don't even think about comin' in without my OK!
Fear the Beard

May 21, 2018

So, we're takin' mom to work down Old Point Road and I'm lookin' out the window for any walkin' canines and dad says, "Better brace yourself, Charley. We're about to run into some weather!"

OMG! What happened to my Plum Island Paradise? **Note from dad**: *When I manipulated this photo, the face became apparent ... at least to me, but then, most of you know me!*

May 21, 2018

Charley here. Dad keeps saying that I look & act like an 'old soul'. So he decided to make my picture look like a 'daguerreotype', whew, I can't even pronounce that!

Dad says the image was captured on a thin piece of silver-plated copper and no negatives so each was unique! Dad says that's what mom and I are but he calls us Uni-Q. Dad is funny! Here I am.

May 26, 2018

It's Charley, friends, at least until I'm in the hoosegow. You see, dad caught me with somethin' in my mouth and he thought it was a stick (dad's eyes are goin', ya know) but then ol' eagle-eye, mom saw there was a fresh bone stickin' outa one end and she thinks it's a bird leg! C'mon friends, she can't tell if any birds are missin', can she? Anyway, it looks like there is gonna be some kinda official inquiry. Can they prosecute if I'm still less than a year old?

Phew, next they will be countin' the bunnies around here! Actually, mom said we should call them rabbits when the grandchildren are around! Gotta go! Here bunny, bunny!

Whaaaat! No way, dad! I haven't seen hide nor hare of any bunnies 'round this yard!

May 30, 2018

Hi friends, it's Charley! I know, it has been a couple of days but I have been busy helpin' dad organize his shop and our new 'Key West' room. That's where me 'n dad go in the morning so he can go out the doggie door to the yard 'n poop and I watch the news! Uh, oh, I think I said that backward! Anyway, I didn't mind helpin' at all!

And I been helpin' to get them flies! Dad laughed the other day 'cause I was stalkin' one and had my front leg up (dad says like a pointer). He missed getting' a picture, tho.

So, dad says I'm getting' a little 'dog-eared' and he is gonna give me a bath this weekend and an 'almost' big dog haircut. I'm getting' my nails done Friday at the vets, Newbury Animal Hospital. Dad says he doesn't do my nails 'cause he doesn't want to hurt me and make the grooming thing a bad experience. Don't worry dad, you can do it. I would forgive you! Anyway here is the 'dog-eared' me! Stay tuned. I'll be 9 months on June 1st!

May 30, 2018

Charley here! I know, twice in one day, but I just had to tell you this. When we get close to home, dad lets me ride in his lap, out the window! Mom says she just loves to watch me bite at the wind and my ears flappin'. She says she can tell how fast we are goin' by nearly imperceptible differences in the pitch of my ears! You know, like you can tell wind speed by how much the trees move. Hey, maybe I'm a speedo-mutt-er! Tee hee hee!

20 MPH!

30 MPH!

CHAPTER 9

June 3, 2018

Charley here! I just got my bath and dad is gonna give me a trim later but I wanted to show you what he did to me. He built me this toybox (it's too little anyway, friends, just sayin') and he really expects me to put my toys in it! Good luck with that dad.

So he said, "I'll fix you, Charley." With that, he buried me in all my toys but soon realized his error 'cause I LOVED it! Well, the toys are back in the toybox but it just ain't workin'. I think I need drawers!

> It's REALLY hard to play with my toys like this, dad!

> Humpfh! It's Murphy's Toybox Law! The thing I want is always at the bottom!

June 4, 2018

Hi everyone, Charley here. Well, here are my new pics after my 'almost big girl' trim. Now that I am 9 months old, dad said he did a little more than the last time but still not 'the works'!

But, you know what friends? I can read my dad like a bone and he wasn't lookin' too happy. What's wrong dad, I asked as I put my paw on his foot, why are you sad? "Well, Charley," he said, "I have been grooming since we had our first Mini Schnauzers, then Lucy, our Standard, who was your predecessor. I have always used an Oster Golden A5 with a #10 blade and a 5/8 blade for close work. Then, when we got you, a 'Pro' said I should be using a 7f blade, and I have been but I don't like the way it leaves your coat. Maybe you could ask your friends what they think?"

So, there it is, friends. Can you help a pup and her dad out? We sure would appreciate the feedback.

June 6, 2018

So, my wonderful friends, dad and I had a really good fight this morning. I mean, I could hardly handle it when he got me on my back and he grabs at my paws and I make believe I'm gonna bite his fingers off. Dad knows I love that! But then he got to my belly (you would think I'd be ready for that move by now!) and he starts tickling! OMG! In seconds we were both laughin' so hard we couldn't breathe!

After we composed ourselves, dad got serious. "Charley," he asked, "now that you are 9 months old, have you been givin' any thought to who you really are?"

Wow, I thought it was gonna be a tough question. Here is what I said:

"I'm a Standard Schnauzer, dad!"

They had a great life, or so they did think.
  Some would say dull, like an old kitchen sink.
They were happy and peaceful, even serene.
  But then I came along and ended that scene.

I was a bundle of love in a puddle of pee
  And Dad said, "She saw right through me."
By definition a dog but, with a human brain,
  Mom and dad thought they were going insane.

We can be black as pitch, like an evening disguise
  And stare with piercing yet vanishing eyes.
But I could be camouflaged by old asphalt.
  Black streaks in white, like pepper 'n salt.

I might stay a puppy for two happy, long years
  And I'll try your patience and bring you to tears.
Tho if you happen to be the Alpha I need,
  I'll learn and play and try to follow your lead.

I'll herd and race and excel at your silly tasks.
  As long as it interests me I'll do what you ask.
And when you return from your labors or sail
  I'll show you my wiggle from shoulders to tail!

I'll guard and protect you, and your children I'll love.
  I will give them my life if push comes to shove.
Remember I'm a warrior and thru bones I might sift,
  Finding you the juiciest to present as a gift!

As I grow brows and beard as only I can
  You may think of me as your wise, old man.
But always remember, if I'm being a wolf or a lamb,
  When all's said 'n done, Standard Schnauzer, I am!

June 9, 2018

Dad says no postin' cause he has to do maintenance, but he's just mad cause I got more likes!

Sorry to disappoint you but it's DAD here! Charley won't be posting today because I have to do maintenance on the internet. I think the internet wire thingy is twisted somewhere and the words can't all get through. So sad.

June 10, 2018

Hi, Friends! I made it back sooner than I thought. Dad fixed the internet. He said that if I type any weird words about him or mom they won't go through the cable and he has to clean them out! Well, guess what, friends. I discovered we have wi-fi! Ha! Try to stop them words, dad!

Anyway, dad really wanted to write somethin' about mom's art. If you want to know who my mom is, you can go here: facebook.com/PlumIslandChuck/posts/1641183092617815

So, friends, as you can see (right), dad and I had a calm, cool and level-headed conversation about this whole computer and Facebook thing. I don't remember his exact words but I'm sure they were somethin' about what a fine, mature young lady I am becoming! See you all soon!

... and ... and I want my own big paws keyboard ... and a touch screen instead of that mouse thing!

June 12, 2018

Hey, gang, Charley here! I've been hearin' mom 'n dad speakin' to each other about how close we have all become. Personally, I don't think they should be surprised. After all, we are a pack, aren't we? Of course, they call us a 'family' and that's fine with me, as long as it means we watch out for & love each other. Hey, isn't that where the term 'puppy love' comes from?

They think it's cute that I panic a little when I come in from outside and dad has gone upstairs, and I dash up to find him, or that I like to lay near mom or dad for security. But I'm a big girl now and they go away for 2 hours and give me the run of the house. Of course, I worry a little but I know they will be back and love me up and be proud of me.

Mom is also surprised when I play with dad and he holds me upside-down and I just relax. I don't get it! Why would I worry? Dad 'n mom are family and would never let me down. I'm so glad I'm the dog with the human brain so I can understand these guys! Nighty-night!

Charley! Hey, Charley! Wake up!!

June 15, 2018

Well, I told you about the great unicorn that Tina Kennedy got me.. So dad showed me the pics on the SS Owners & Breeders site about my friends, like MacKenzey (Happy Birthday, MacKenzy!) and Kai with their babies.

'Course I got Twinky (that's what I call her now) when I was just a kid, but I still carry her around. Dad got me Finky, (I think I'm partial to 'girl' friends! That's what I call Finkle Fox, get it, Twinky & Finky). I was actually accused of doin'-in Finky Fox but it was a bum rap. I had witnesses that I was just tryin' to resuscitate him when they found me mouthin' him! Phew!

March 2018

I went right to my hangout to snuggle with "Twinkle Fancy Face".

Yes, we're goin' upstairs. All of a sudden we feel surrounded by paparazzi!

June 2018

This is my BFF Twinkle!

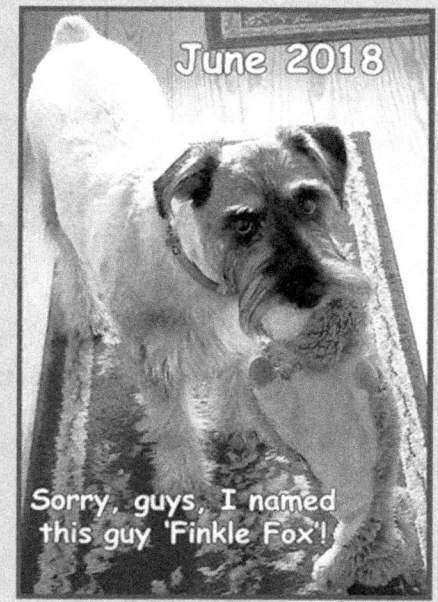

June 2018

Sorry, guys, I named this guy 'Finkle Fox'!

June 18, 2018

Hi friends, it's Charley. Well, it's been a tough couple of days but first I'm just gonna post a picture of a life lesson I learned!

PUPPY MATH

1 Playful Puppy + 1 Hot & Humid Day + 1 Senior Citizen 85 Lb. Dog − 1 Sense of Knowing When to Quit = 1 Punctured Puppy

Charley

June 18, 2018

It's Charley, friends! So, I'm sure my puppy buddies out there will agree with me that it is sooo fun to do the ol' in 'n out, the nip 'n tuck and the strike 'n dodge with them older dogs, right? I mean, they tolerate us, right? Well, nobody ever told me there was a limit!

Here I was, havin' the time of my life and all of a sudden I gets a bark. OK I think, lets add some interest to this game. Then there was a pretty serious growl! Now I'm thinkin', hey, that's how to play the game … so I give him my best Schnauzer bark and growl. There, right back at ya! Well, friends, that's when he hit me! I didn't even think he could move that fast but before I could say, beat ya to the treats, he put a rather large hole in my thigh! I hardly noticed and kept playin' but later, when we got home, mom noticed I wasn't quite right. Then she saw the hole, screamed a blood-curdling scream and fainted into dads arms. No, I'm just kiddin'. Dad actually, accidentally put his finger in the hole when he was checkin' my leg this mornin'.

Then, it was to the vet, get stapled like last years tax return and take some meds. But, I've learned my less … wait, look, I see that Shepard in the other yard. Be right back.

June 18, 2018 cont.

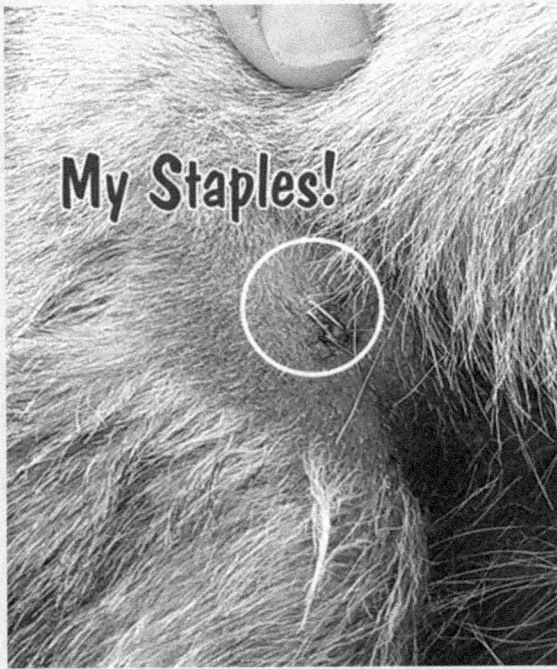

My Staples!

Don't tell mom, but dad says it's kinda cool to have some battle scars.

June 18, 2018 cont.

Hey friends, Charley here. Thanks for all of your well wishes and advice. I'm feelin' back to my ol' self already! Dad says he's not sure that is a good thing. I saw him sittin' on the edge of his chair with his head in his hands and I think he mumbled "two more years of puppyhood". Dad has a funny way of showin' he's happy!

Hey, does anyone know a good bloodhound I can get to help me? Mom & dad gave me these things today and they were great chewin' and refreshin'. I like fishin' them out of my bowl and blowin' bubbles in it! But I'm tellin' you, I ate a couple of them things and left the other one for later and when I came back, it was GONE! Then it happened again later. Every time I leave one, it is gone when I go back for it! I need some help here, friends!

Mom 'n dad laugh when I put my face in here & make bubbles!

OK! I ate two & I'm savin' this for later.

June 21, 2018

Well, friends, I was startin' to feel bad 'cause dad said I wasn't catchin' enough bugs. Believe me, I'm tryin' hard! But then I felt really special when he said I was a brave girl for not even flinchin' when he uses those big saws and shop vacuum and all. And, to top it off he was proud of me when I started to bark at that thunder & lightenin' stuff. Why, heck, it doesn't scare me!

Anyway, I helped him make 2 of (what dad calls) Kup Kaps! They are just for his mug to keep the bugs out and he put pictures of his two favorite girls on them. I sure love dad!

Dad added a piece so it won't slide off!

June 28, 2018

Hey, friends! Well, I think I have told you before how much of a 'hard case' dad is in the trainin' area. I mean, I bend over backward tryin' to make life easy for him and it's like I'm barkin' up the wrong tree! Now, mom, on the other paw, just 'gets it' but dad, oh, boy!

So, they have been feedin' me this Wellness food cause dad researched it for quality and all. But, every now 'n then I get a carrot or a piece of apple and I even like spinach! So, I've been (I guess the word is pesterin') dad for veggies. Well, you know us Standards. We have our standards and one of them is to worry an issue 'til it bites us or we win!

Finally, dad throws this thing on the floor and says, "Here, Charley, some veggies for you"!

Yeah, friends, I guess I had it comin'!

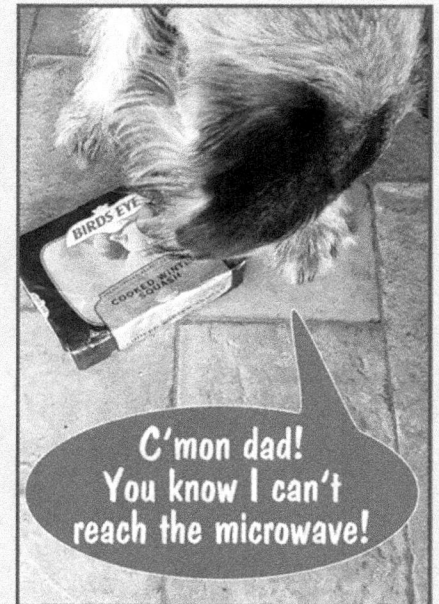

C'mon dad! You know I can't reach the microwave!

A dog teaches a boy fidelity , perseverance, and to turn around three times before lying down .

Robert Benchley

June 29, 2018

How DAD sees dad!

Hi friends. I really need to write to get my mind off things! Dad has been actin' crazy all day and he's makin' mom & I crazy too!

It all started with dad announcin' this mornin', before we even got our eyes open, mind you, that this was not another black Friday with sales and everythin', but a truly BLACK Friday 'cause Toys R Us is shuttin' its doors! With that announcement, he began singin' "I don't wanna grow up … I'm a Toys R Us kid", over 'n over!

OMG! Mom says it's OK & just smiles! She has said repeatedly that dad is 73 goin' on 14 and possibly has alien blood in him. Well, now I believe her! C'mon, I want my dad back – the guy with 2 phony knees, a bi-lateral laminotomy and who gets a needle in his eye every month! That is unless … unless… he shares some of that ice cream cone with me. Hmmmm.

What dad REALLY looks like!

Note from dad: I may have to take some privileges away from this little girl!

Another note from dad: I DO NOT HAVE A WHEELCHAIR! A recliner isn't the same thing!

CHAPTER 10

July 1, 2018

> Hey, mom, dad built this deck rail at just the right height for guardin'!

Hi friends! Well, my dad has done it again. I realized this morning that when he built our back deck he made the rail just the right height! Now I can guard the back of the house and not get tired. I may have pushed it a little too far when I off-handedly asked if he has ever seen anything like a 'doggie lounge chair'.

Anyway, this morning we were all sittin' and guardin' when we heard Louise Murphy's Riley bark. I just let it go but not dad. Dad let go a few high-pitched barks and got Riley goin'. Personally, I thought it was funny but mom gave dad the 'look' and Sunday morning became peaceful once again.

July 1, 2018

Hey, friends! Charley here! I know, I know, 2 posts today, but I really have to explain a picture that mom took. You know, I don't look in the mirror much and when I do I don't open my mouth, or smile (like I've seen dad do). So, when I saw this pic it even scared me! I can't believe the size of them choppers I have! Rest assured, I'm NOT attackin' dad!

We play this game a lot, especially in the mornin' when he isn't quite awake and I can get a few good licks in. Dad grabs my feet and tickles my belly and (I've said it before) we start laughin' til our eyes start leakin' and our bellies hurt.

That's my story, and I'm stickin' to it!

July 2, 2018

Hey friends, Charley here. Well, you all know by now that I sure do love mom 'n dad. Of course, dad and I have had our differences lately but I just attribute those to (dad's) growin' pains. I mean, all families have their differences, right? Dad actually threatened to take away my postin' time! So, you can imagine how shocked and pleased I was when dad came downstairs and showed me his new T-shirt. It said "Chuck and Charley", with dad's and my picture. Then dad said he would make one for me!

Well, girlfriends, OMG! I don't even get top billin'! So I suggested to dad, "How about mine sayin' Charley 'n dad"? Well, while dad was ponderin' I ran upstairs and grabbed one of dad's shirts that I could really live with.

I threw it on and ran downstairs (almost breakin' my neck in all that fabric) and said, "Dad, how about this in my size"? Then he just put his head in his hands and I think I heard a moan. The jury is still out!

(In case you can't read it, it says, "Please don't make me do stuff".)

July 3, 2018

Hi friends, Charley here. Well, I keep hearin' these names thrown out there. Twain, Holly, and Lucy, it turns out, were my predecessors (Dad says it means they were here before me). When I found out about that, I wanted to know all about them. So, dad found some pictures on the computer and showed them to me.

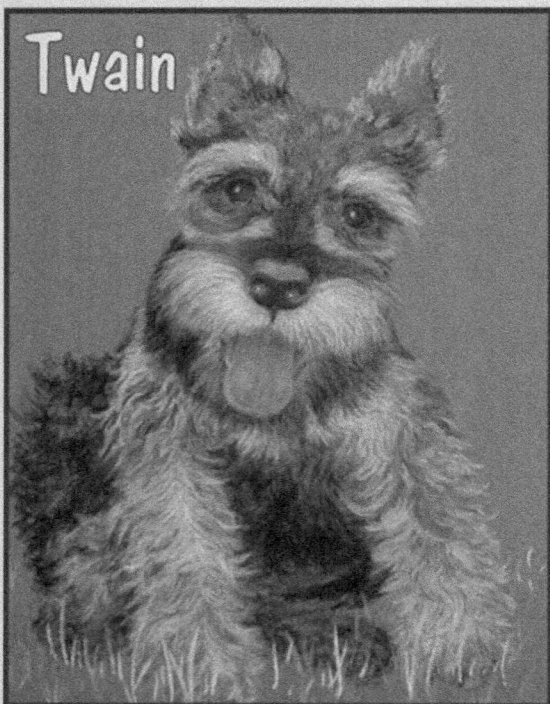

He said Twain was a Mini Schnauzer who thought he was a Standard Schnauzer. He was dad,s first real dog and he was 38 pounds. Dad says he kept tellin' the vet that Twain was 'big-boned'. One of the pictures of Twain is a pastel that mom did when he was a pup.

Then there was Holly, also a Mini and she was, dad says, really sweet. They got her to keep Twain company when everyone was at work and she was

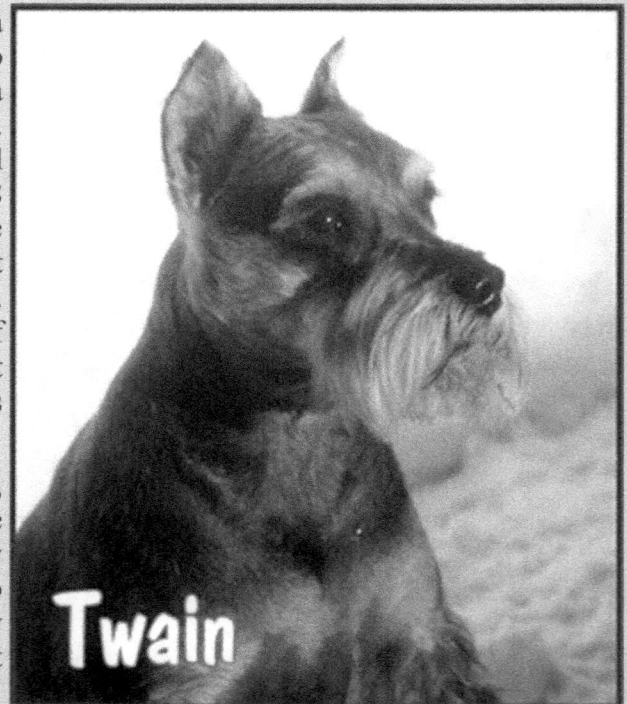

technically mom's dog. But dad says Holly was tryin' on their nerves 'cause she was a yipper, whatever that means.

Finally, there was Lucy, er, wait, I guess I'm 'finally, but Lucy (one of her pics is a watercolor dad did on the computer) was before me. Dad says they didn't know to look up a good breeder for Standard Schnauzers and Lucy passed on at 7 years old. It sounds like they really loved Lucy and all of the others 'cause dad started to tear up a bit when he talked about them. He turned away from me, but I could tell.

And, oh yeah, dad said they found me at a great breeder, Shalimar's Standard Schnauzers in Angola, NY.

Holly

Lucy

Lucy

LUIZ

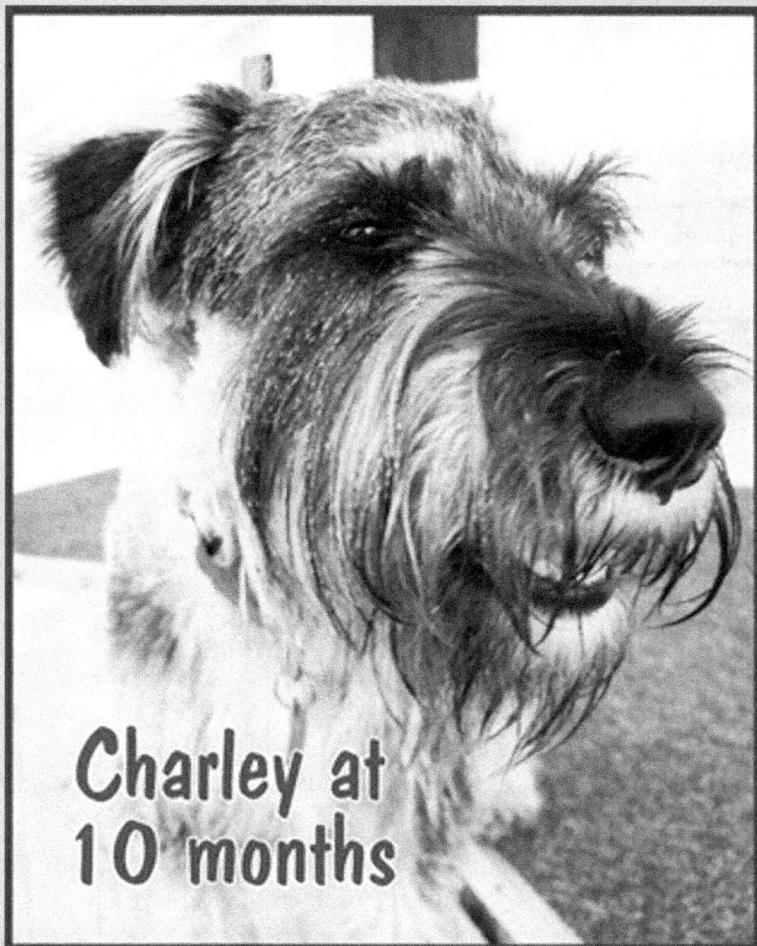

Charley at 10 months

Notes from dad: Pat did the pastel of Twain when he was a pup! Twain was almost regal (and acted like it). He was the best. He was big but all muscle. When I got him into the water, he could hardly swim. Hence, dog-paddle. Holly was the sweetheart of Mini Schnauzers. Lucy could do no wrong. She was the love of our lives and will always hold a special place in our hearts and I really enjoyed doing the watercolor on the computer!

July 5, 2018

It looked like a big water bowl to me!

Hi friends, it's Charley. So, it's been really hot and humid these last few days at our Plum Island Paradise! I was layin' on the cool, tile kitchen floor when I hear mom callin' me from out back.

BTW, I always run when mom calls 'cause it means somethin' good or at least some lovin'-up! On the other paw, I never know with dad, so I might ease into the come thing while I check his hands for a leash or a brush or a pill bottle! Anyway, I gets outside and they are puttin' water into this big green thing. It looked like a huge water bowl to me so I started drinkin' as fast as I could. OMG! I was fillin' up fast! You know, they're old so maybe they think I'm a duck or somethin'!

Then dad started playin' with the hose thing and squirtin' it at me! That was fun for a while but soon he picked me up and then (another OMG 'cause you won't believe it) put me IN THE WATER BOWL!! Then he started splashin' me with water! I thought the ol' man has finally lost his marbles and I would be in trouble.

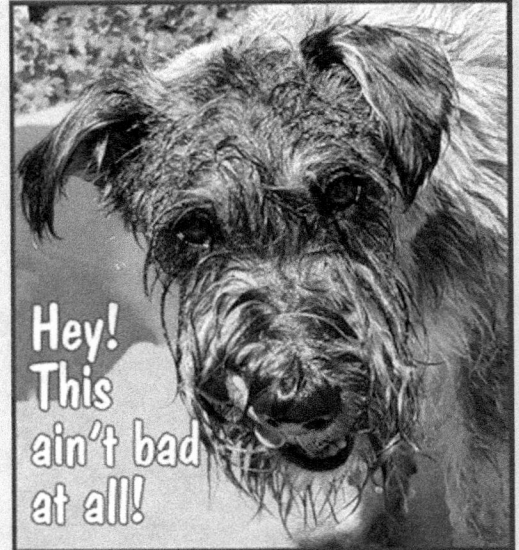

Hey! This ain't bad at all!

Well, it turns out that that thing is meant to get wet in! We were all laughin' and havin' fun … that is, until I jumped out of the water bowl, ran through the dirt and zipped into the house. Wow, hope we do that again tomorrow! PS: For the record, I was NOT afraid of those fireworks! After I barked at them I just happened to be really comfy between dads legs and the chair!

July 5, 2018

For the love of God, dad, how long are you gonna nurse that drink?

Hi friends, it's Charley again! Well, I am enjoyin' the summer as much as possible. My human brother, Erik came by today with my sister-in-law, Tanya. We gave them some of dad's chili 'cause they have been travelin' to see my cousin Kyle's graduation from the Air Force basic trainin'! It was great to see them but I sure do miss Kyle. Me 'n dad 'n mom have been writin' but it's just not the same.

I didn't even get to taste the chili 'cause dad said it is too spicy for, get this, my little puppy belly! Sure, dad! It's probably ruined by you ticklin' it so much! Just kiddin', dad, I don't want you to stop.

These Poland Springs Sparkling Water bottles arethe best … especially lemon!

So, friends, I have discovered the best, by far, interestin' chewy thingy! They call it a, get this, a bottle! Dad says he invented it to drink stuff from and so I could play with it! But … but… when I looked over at mom, she was shakin' her head like she was watchin' tennis. I've figured out that when she does that dad may be doin' what she calls 'embellishin'. Anyway, these things are the most fun ever. The ones for plain water, not so much. They just crush up too easy. But, those Poland Springs sparklin' water bottles pop right outta my teeth and go flyin' and then I chase it and they make a racket too! WOW 'n OMG, this is great!

But, I heard mom yesterday say to dad, "Charley, (she calls him Charley instead of Chuckie when she has the 'look'), look at all those toys and how much we spent, and she (that's me, I think) loves those plastic bottles!" I think I'll leave it at that!

July 12, 2018

Hey friends, Charley here. Well, I really ain't feelin' a post today. Dad has been hoggin' the computer lately. He's been postin' some pictures of Newburyport and he writes some poignant (wow, I didn't even know I know that word!) and he even writes some of that poetry stuff. So I asked him to take a 10 month pic and he did so here it is.

Between you 'n me, his pics are old as the hills. Good thing! His short-term memory is shot! Why, I think he only remembers my name is Charley 'cause it's his name too ... uh, oh, I think I'm in trouble ... gotta go!

July 16, 2018

C'mon Charley, take the pill and you can have the treat!

Hi, Charley here friends. Well, it has been an interesting few days around here It all started when I did my Schnauzer puppy speed grab when dad had the door to under the house open for a couple of minutes. I really hit the jackpot! I brought one treasure upstairs and that night dad heard it hit the floor and put it on the table. The next morning, when dad looked at what it was, he got this worried look on his face, like the time I ran down our street and wouldn't listen when he called me!

Turns out it was somethin' called D-Con. Yeah, a tasty little green block that I heard dad tell the vet was used for feedin' mice. Well, why should them mice have all the fun?

So, to make a short story even shorter, dad got a 'scription for somethin' called vitamin K1. Dad says it's so I won't bleed. Well, I know how not to bleed – just stay away from sharp stuff, right? I have to take 1 of these twice a day and dad was very impressed with how I can spit them out. I could even get the peanut butter off and spit that pill right out! So now, dad just 'neeks up on me and sticks it right down my throat and holds my mouth shut. I sure would like to give him a little nip, but I won't 'cause ...'cause ... well 'cause he's dad! See you all soon!

July 19, 2018

Hi, friends, Charley here. Well, things are goin' well for 3 or 4 days now here at our Plum Island Paradise. There have been no more Standard Schnauzer 'incidents'. I really don't know why they make a big deal out of them. After all, it was just a little bite I got and how did I know that green thing was bad. I agree with my FB pals, dad should have hidden it better!

Dad says that was 2 things and he is waitin' for the other shoe to drop. I didn't see the first one and, believe me, I would have been on it!

Let's look at the bright side! I haven't bitten dad when he gives me the pill. Tuesday, when that lightenin' hit in our yard, I ran out to 'get it'. And, even though dad plays real hard with Auntie Cheryl's Christmas moose she gave me, I haven't 'accidentally' nipped him! Yup, I'm doin' GREAT!

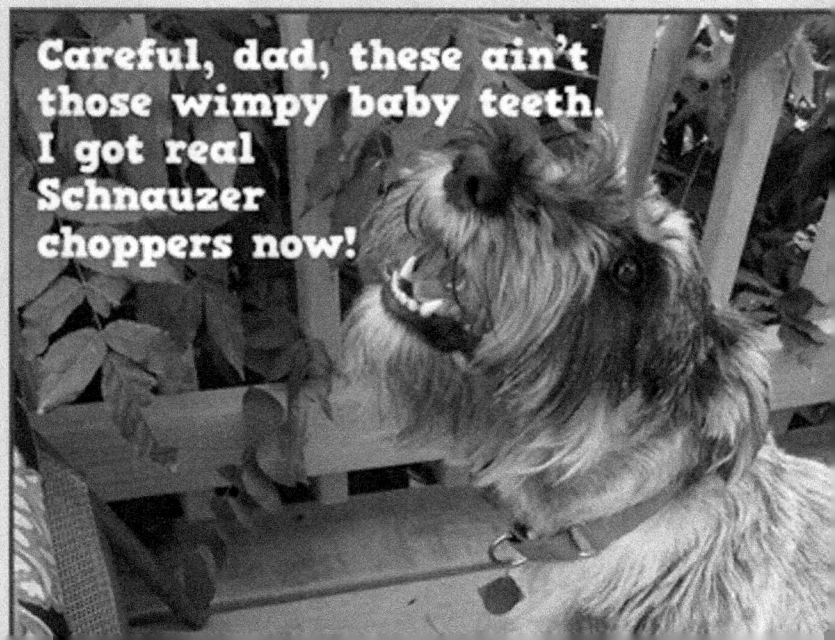

Careful, dad, these ain't those wimpy baby teeth. I got real Schnauzer choppers now!

July 22, 2018

Hi friends, Charley here! Well, it's been a nice, laid-back weekend here at Plum Island Paradise. Yesterday, dad threw a couple of steaks on the grill and made mashed potatoes, broccoli and gravy. It was one of my favorite meals 'cause I get to lick dad's plate when he is done. Dad left a little too much gravy and he wasn't sure about givin' it all to me. I think he was mostly worried 'bout wipin' my beard when I was done! I think that's why he doesn't give me his plate after a meal involvin' tomato sauce.

Speakin' of food, I haven't been a real happy puppy at meal time. Mom 'n dad already feed me once a day 'cause I'm just not hungry in the mornin'. Dr. Grillo said it's OK. On the other paw, I'm not overjoyed with their food choices for me. Dad likes to give me mostly kibble (cause he says it's good for chewin'), mixed with some wet food. He is really a big fan of Wellness Core but he was tryin' some less 'spensive food. I didn't like them much at all. Then, the other day, he bought me some 'RawRev'. I liked that, especially with the Wellness 95% Chicken. But dad says the can part costs 3.49 each at the pet store! I'm really thinkin' I like raw food. Do any of my pals out there have any suggestions?

July 23, 2018

Charley here, friends. So, I've been doin' a lot of car ridin' lately. Mom 'n dad told me that Lucy used to be a little afraid to ride in the car. They loved Lucy a lot and I wish we could have met 'cause I think I would have loved her too. Anyway, I think the car is the best invention since the beaches! I can sit on mom 'n dad's laps, stick out my head and bite that wind, and sometimes sit on dad's lap and bite the wind at the same time when he's drivin'! (He only lets me do that for the last little ways before our driveway 'cause he says the policeman might not be happy about it). Mostly, I like to put my front paws right between dad 'n mom so I can see everything. Dad says I am doin' great at leanin'. He says, "Left turn!, Right turn! Stoppin! or Here we go!" I'm learnin' to lean or brace myself. Boy, drivin' is sure fun! Well, except sometimes when dad yells, "Charley! I can't see out the passenger window!"

July 24, 2018

DAD! C'mon dad, where did you put the black 'n white toy?

So, here we were this mornin', friends, in our Plum Island Paradise basement room (Mom 'n dad call it Key West). Dad 'n I go there every morning and I go out the doggie door and poop (I'm supposed to call it, doin' my business). Well, I looked out to the yard and there was a new toy for me! It was black 'n white and MOVIN'! WOW!

So out I go at top speed and got ready for some fun. Then, louder than I have ever heard him, dad yelled, "Charley, NO!" Dad was out the door faster than I thought he could move and he told me to go upstairs the other way and he made me go inside. I really wanted to play but I have learned to listen to dad so off I went.

Then I heard dad talkin' to mom about how glad he was that I listened to him. Well, hello … he's dad!

I've been out since and I can't figure out what he did with my toy. Maybe he is hidin' it 'til later!

July 26, 2018

Guess what? I got to spend time with mom at her art school, The Artists Playground, yesterday! Dad went to Quinn's Canine Café, just down the hall, to get me some of her delish liver treats so I got to hang out with mom.

I've been there lots of times but sometimes I can't go in. Like durin' the summer there are kid's camps and there are maybe 30 kids from 8 to 11 years old. Dad told mom a formula. 30 Kids + 11 month old Schnauzer = bedlam. I don't know that word but my dad's a genius so it must be right!

But … but I DO get to go in when dad picks up mom on Tuesday night. They are all my buddies and they play with me at the end of class. I call them my Tuesday girlfriends! There's Tina, Lisa, Kathy, Linda, Mary and a couple others. Oh, yeah, there is also Colin but he is usually gone early so I don't get to maul … er, play with him. Too bad, 'cause he has a puppy too and he smells really good. See ya!

Now … where does mom keep those colored pencils? I'm gonna start a class on the ART of chewin'!

July 28, 2018

Hi friends, Charley here! So, I got this wonderful reveal from mom yesterday! I just assumed (silly me) that my friends are all Schnauzers Then mom tells me that their human partners (dad calls them soulmates) are my friends too! Who knew? I just went into an uncontrollable wiggle butt 'cause I am so happy!

Anyway, (and this is for my SS buds) do you have this uncontrollable love for cheese? OMG, I thought I died and went to pup-heaven! I mean, I don't care what kind; blue, Swiss, cheddar and especially Gruyère. Dad says I have expensive taste. (By the way, some of you said to put my pill in liverwurst. YUK! I'd rather eat the pill!)

So, yesterday, dad made what he calls his 'signature' dish, Baked Mac 'n Cheese à la Chuckie. (Don't even get me started on a 73-year-old man bein' called 'Chuckie'! You should hear some of the other endearments they have for each other. It's embarrassin' I tell ya.)

To make a long story short, I hung out in the kitchen for a long time, waitin' to give dad a paw if needed. There were some 'accidental drops'. At one point, dad left that dish really close to the edge of the counter – but I was a good girl!

Dad, don't forget, if you need any help, any help at all, with that HUGE dish of Mac 'n Cheese, I'll lend a paw!

July 31, 2018

Charley here! Well, we had a bit of a party on the weekend at my brother Erik's house. All our relatives from Indiana were there. Their names are … hmmm … are, I got it Jen, Connor, Megan, Fiona, Gillian and Owen, whew! That Owen sure can wear a puppy out! Their Alpha male, Dan, couldn't make it but I hope I'll see him next year. Also there was Augie's family (you remember Augie, don't you?), Chris, Trisha, Emma and Eliza! There was also, of course, Erik, Tanya and Kate (bein' it was their house) and Nancy and Roland. I may have a pic tomorrow! All I can say is it was a great time. It was sooo tirin' tryin' to jump up on so many folks! I kept tryin' to score some of dad's Mac 'n Cheese I wrote about but no luck. Dad has let me lick his plate at home since then!

It was all great fun but I was sad that Kyle wasn't able to be there 'cause he just finished Air Force Basic trainin' and now is in another school. I love Kyle and can't wait to see him again!

So, getting' to me, I have discovered I like lookin' down from high places. This picture is me on my front deck where I can peruse all visitors and decide who gets in. The other day I got in trouble with mom 'cause I tried to keep Julie, our mail human, out. Turns out she was deliverin' a couple of important packages and one was food for me! But she just pushed her way thru the gate anyway and said, "Hi, Charley!" She must be one of those psychic humans like that dog whisperin' guy. Anyway, I won't try keepin' her out again, that's for sure! See you soon!

CHAPTER 11
August 1, 2018

Hi, friends! This is another pic from the aforementioned party. It isn't the greatest, but I wanted to show you 'cause I love my cousins Eliza (in this pic) and Emma! Hope to show you more of them 'n me in a couple of weeks.

Would you believe dad was a Copley photographer and used to teach it for a while when they first opened the art school? I was gonna ask him to teach me to take selfies but now I'm not so sure. Uh, oh! Here he comes! Gotta go!

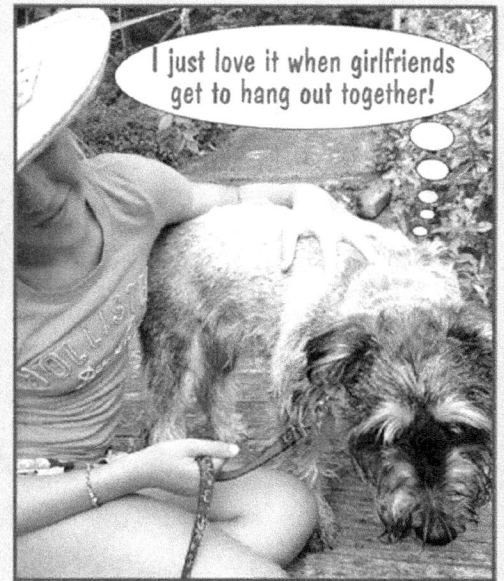

I just love it when girlfriends get to hang out together!

August 1, 2018

Hey, friends, Charley again. Dad 'n me are about to go to Newbury Animal Hospital. Oh, I'm fine, but dad likes to take me there to see all my girlfriends and to get my nails trimmed. Dad grooms me but he doesn't like to cut my nails. He says they are so black and he is havin' a harder time seein' and he doesn't want to hurt me! Hey, that works for me! I'm gonna ask for pink polish! He also took some pictures this morning 'cause it's my 11 month birthday! He said he want's them for that paws-terity thing. Anyway, I tried to stay still. Then he told me to look up to heaven for a side view. I'm not sure what that is yet so I looked up to where they keep my treats. I think it is close to heaven! Finally, dad played around with that art thing on the computer to make me look like a watercolor. I can't wait for him to teach me that program! Can you imagine the troub, er, fun I could have! Bye.

I don't know about heaven, dad, but up there are where the treats are!

August 1, 2018

Charley here, girls! Well, I just got my nails done but I was pretty upset. Turns out, there was no pink polish, only blue, or so they said! So I was sulkin' in the car, you know, like only us Standard Schnauzers can do. Dad asked me where I got the 'attitude' and when did I become such a 'Diva'? (does that mean goin' under water?).

Anyway, when we got home, dad let me wear mom's Bermuda hat with the anchor on it! I love that hat 'cause I make believe it says Plum Island Paradise on it! See ya soon!

August 2, 2018

Hi friends, a steamin' Charley here! We had a couple of dry days here on Plum Island in northeastern Massachusetts (how do they expect a little girl to spell THAT?), but now it getting' muggy, with a vengeance!

Mom 'n dad always make sure I have plenty of cold water and sometimes dad puts some ice cubes in it. He likes to watch me 'divin' for cubes', as he calls it, and blowin' bubbles under water. I have to admit, I love it too!

Mom told me that dad is gonna start hidin' my nighttime treats. Mom says he used to hide Lucy's treats in very difficult places and she always found them. Dad says Standard Schnauzers need to be challenged more than most other dogs so we can use our almost 'human brain'. He's right! I hate bein' bored! But, between you 'n me, friends, I think dad hates bein' bored more than me! Just sayin'!

Oh, yeah, about this picture. We were sittin' on the front porch and dad was drinkin' a Poland Springs Sparklin' Water. Well, it bein' so hot, he put a little in a cup for me. Boy was that cold 'n tasty! But, when I jumped up for more, he said, sorry, Charley, only a taste! He said if I had too much carbonated stuff it could give me gas and I could get real sick. He won't give me caffeine, grape juice, smoothies with yogurt or avocado in it or any kind of chocolate drink. Dad says some folks think animals can eat what they eat and it isn't true. Well, I love dad and I trust whatever he tells me. See ya!

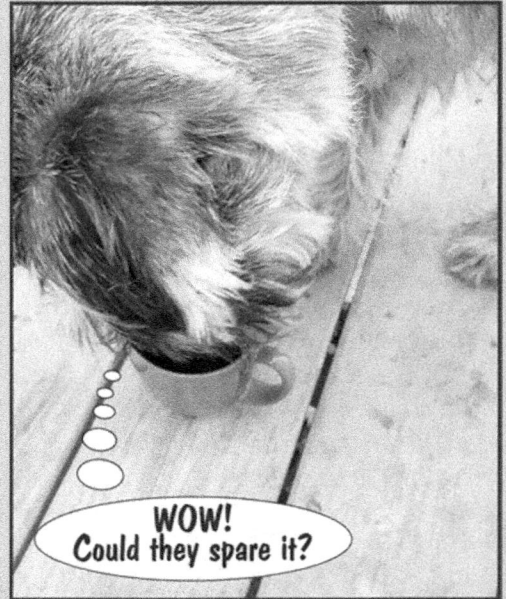

WOW!
Could they spare it?

August 2, 2018

Note from dad: I saw this before Charley posted it. Hope you all don't mind the post. I told her this is a SS group, not for humans. She promised not to do it again!

Hi friends, Charley again, on the same day! I just couldn't wait to show you some new pack photographs.

So, here I am takin' some shots around the house with dad's phone and mom 'n dad were sittin' havin' a serious conversation 'bout what to have for dinner.

[By the way, I've pretty much settled on my dry food, Wellness RawRev. Dad has been tryin' some new toppers and we are getting' there. He did mention somethin' 'bout me getting' a part-time job to help pay for this food.]

Anyway, after I put a plug in for grilled meat, any meat, I said, hey, I don't have any good pictures of my mom 'n dad! Would you pose for me? They said sure but they didn't know I found a 'stickers' button on the phone and it let me picture them just like I see them!

August 3, 2018

Charley here and it's a big day at Plum Island Paradise. Recently, when dad and I get downstairs to Key West, he goes outside first and I think he checks the weather. He has been doin' this ever since the black 'n white toy was around. Then he lets me out through my special Schnauzer door. Dad took my picture this morning. He said it was a 'screen test', whatever that is. He was smirkin' a little so I think he was pullin' my paw! You never know with dad! So, then I am on the hunt for some big game. You wouldn't believe the furry and feathered neighbors I have on this island. Part of the island is the Parker River National Wildlife Refuge, which should tell you somethin'. Dad says the wildlife isn't as smart as us Schnauzers and don't know to stay in their refuge.

Anyway, dad says he has seen coyote, fox, fisher, skunk, possum, rabbit, red-tailed hawk, falcon and eagles. He said he's caught skunks and relocated them. I asked if he took a picture and he said he did but it stunk. I think he is foolin' with me. 'Night, friends. It's been a long day. Think I'll do some downtime with Twinky.

August 4, 2018

Hey, gang, Charley here. Mom 'n dad got me the greatest thing ever, yesterday! They call it a Rumba bone or marrow bone. I call it delicious! There is a tiny bit of raw meat on the outside but on the inside is this wonderful stuff! I almost have it all out now and I hate to see it end but I saw dad get this out of a package with other ones so I am keepin' my toes crossed! He says I am gonna 'worry' it. Nope. I'm just worried I won't get another one!

Sorry dad, if you wanted to play you shouldn't have given me this BONE!

August 5, 2018

I know those little buggers are in there but they won't come out 'n fight!

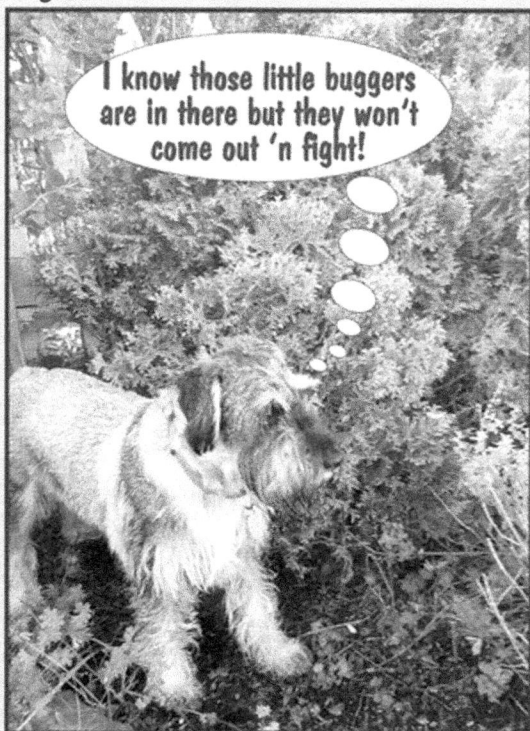

Hi friends, it's Charley. Yesterday was a tough day for the most part! I spent all morning in the deep jungle, chasin' those darn elusive white flutterin' things. Wow, are they hard to catch! I think my little puppy neck got whiplash tryin' to keep track of them.

Mom 'n dad were no help at all. They just sat there drinkin' their iced coffee and stayin' cool! I think I even heard a few snickers but I can't be sure. Dad tried to help, in a way. He yelled, "Hey, Charley, I'm gonna buy you a butterfly net!" Yeah, thanks dad, but you keep forgetin' about the 'opposin' thumbs' thing!

Savannah 'n me.

Then, my day got so much better. Our neighbors' (Susan 'n Frank) daughter and granddaughter were here for a visit Well, I have never met Savannah before. She is five years old and you all know how much I LOVE little children! The only thing is I get Sooo excited that I asked dad to keep me on my tether thingy so I wouldn't knock Savannah over. Susan asked me to smile and I did my best! But it was great to meet you Savannah! I love you!

August 5, 2018

Well friends, I think I'm losin' it! Dad got this awesome gift from what I call the 'Tuesday Night Girls +1'. Dad was all excited when he opened it and he showed it to me. Well! and OMG! You coulda' knocked me over with a Milkbone! There, lookin' back at me was a Schnauzer! I was pretty sure it was one of me or one of them Mini's so I gave 'im the old sniff test. (You know we originated the 'scratch 'n sniff' test, don't you?).

This is where it gets interestin', friends. I couldn't get a single puppy odor! Nothin'! All I could get was overwhelmin' human, and I think it was that Tina girl! Now I'm thinkin', SECRET GOVERNMENT PROJECT! Maybe they have designed the 'stealth' dog!

Anyway, dad seemed to love it and he put it on the shelf where he can see it all the time. That's nice for dad, but now, hello, those little puppy eyes are followin' me whenever I am in the room. Thanks, TNG's+1, but you are responsible if I grow up puparanoid!

August 6, 2018

Hi everyone, Charley here. Well, don't tell dad, but our Plum Island Paradise has become our Plum Island Hothouse! They don't like to use those air conditionin' (dad has one in his room but he says it is for the *computer equipment*! Hmmmm?) so we have a lot of fans. I finally figured out how those things work 'cause I walked past one of them and whoowee! It gave me a little start, I'll tell you. Then one time I was goin' in front of it and I stopped to scratch. Well, I thought, this might be the place to hang out!

Dad was watchin' me and he said I could be in his 'fan club'. I've learned a valuable lesson for a young, impressionable pup … when dad says somethin' weird, I look over at mom. If she doesn't react at all I'm good to go. If she gets that little smirk and maybe shakes her head, then I have to take what dad is sayin' with a grain of kibble! But, if she looks up to the ceilin' I have to brace myself for all possibilities!

Anyway, between them fans and those cold things I'm survivin'. Now I'm not leavin' them cold things 'til I finish em. 'Member I told you before when dad gave me one it just disappeared when I left it to do somethin' else. Never again, friends!!

No way I'm leavin' this one till I'm done!

August 7, 2018

So, friends, I scored another one of those Rumba marrow bones today. Those things are incredible! I think that dad said he was gonna give me one when he gets home but mom beat him to the punch. Yea, mom! I tried to get mom to not mention this little thing to dad but he caught me with it anyway.

Now, let me ask my Schnauzer buds out there, don't you try to bury your bones? Mom was all aghast when I took it and dug a hole in that nice, soft loam 'n mulch in the garden and dropped that marrow bone in it. I took it back out again and started chewin' it but mom didn't think it was very appetizin' with all that black dirt on it. I think it's like the stuff she calls breadin'!

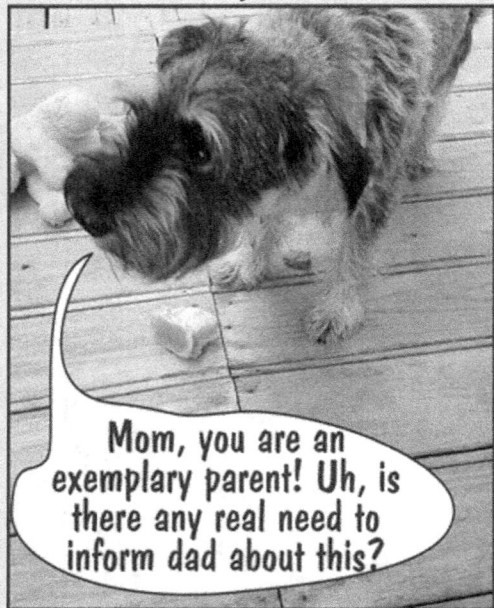

Then mom told me a story about my predecessor, Lucy. She used to bring a bone and put it next to dad in his seat. Then she moved her nose like she was coverin' it up. Then she jumped down, mom says very pleased with herself., and go about her business. Mom says the bone was right there, next to dad, but apparently, Lucy considered it to be safe there. Well, gotta go. Mom 'n dad are startin' to hide my treats. I usually know where they are but I play along so they'll feel good!

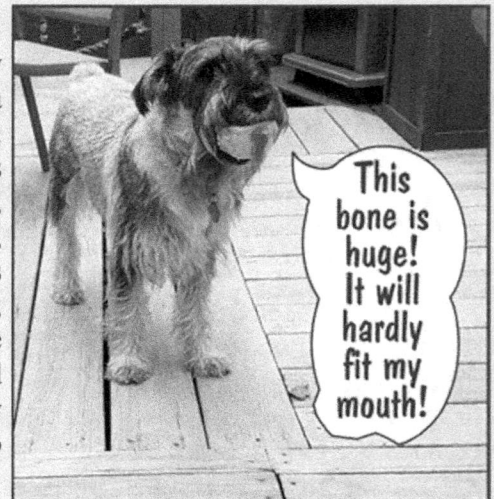

Mom, you are an exemplary parent! Uh, is there any real need to inform dad about this?

This bone is huge! It will hardly fit my mouth!

August 8, 2018

Charley here, friends! Well, let me tell you, I have to be careful of that dad of mine 'cause he could sure get me in trouble! We usually all go out to the back deck in the mornin' 'cause it's cooler there and dad might bring me a liver treat that he gets from Quinn's Canine Café. (I love them treats!)

So, dad 'n me are out on the deck but mom wasn't there yet. Dad tells me to put Twinky on mom's chair and we'll make believe it's her. Then dad whispers to me to ask mom if I can sleep and play on her new comforter. So I did, and then dad answers in a high-pitched voice, 'Sure, Charley, you can do anything you want on that comforter!" Well, dad started laughin' and he got me laughin' so much our bellies hurt! Then I realized mom was just in the other room and could hear us. She came outside with her 'not happy face' on. I took Twinky and ran all the way to the front yard. I don't know what happened to dad! See ya!

Mom

C'mon Twinkle! I hear mom comin'. We'll both be in trouble!

August 10, 2018

So, friends, here I was on our P.I.P. back deck, just kinda hangin' out and makin' sure no intruders got in. Then, OMG! This thing came swoopin' out'a nowhere! Swoopin' I tell ya! It was sort of like those other ones that tease me in the yard. They let me 'neek up on them and all of a sudden they stretch out those funny lookin' arms and jump higher than you can imagine. I try but I can't jump like them. Then dad told me they are birds and they do a thing called flyin'! Wow! I'm gonna practice 'til I can do that! It sure looks fun!

But, this thing never hit the ground. It just swooped up to the top of that pole and stood there, starin' at me. I gave him my best bark and a few growls but he wouldn't leave. So, I just held my ground! Dad says it was a Plum Island Stand-off! Well, with all the ruckus, mom 'n dad came out and dad went back inside to get his good camera. By the time he came back, it had become too afraid of me and fled the scene! Of course, I told mom 'n dad there was no need to thank me!

Yo! Keep that Charley away from me!

Old Eagle Eye on I Street Plum Island!

You can come out dad! He ain't comin' back on my watch!

August 11, 2018

So, my wonderful, faithful, loving, supportive friends! I need your help! Mom 'n dad are gangin' up on me! They have this crazy idea in their heads that I am lookin' 'dog-eared' and I need this thing called groomin' periodically! Hey, I can do my own groomin', thank you! A little scratch here, a little scratch there and a couple full-body, moisture shakes and I'm done! Oh, Noooo! They have other ideas!

Yup! They have this irrational need for the bathtub, shampoo, dryer and then puttin' me on that table dad built (that I'm not crazy about anyway) and then usin' that huge lawnmower thingy to shave off that which has taken me so long to grow back from the last time!

C'mon friends, tell dad I should keep the natural, wild 'n wooly look of a Schnauzer!

At least dad is considerin' my request to do my bath in that big green water bowl outside. It won't be 'til Monday or Tuesday 'cause it is pretty rainy here on Plum Island this weekend. Dad says he wants me to look 'pretty' for my 1-year old birthday party on September 1st. YUK!

August 12, 2018

Hi, friends. Charley here! Well, it's been one heck of a wet one for the past couple days and it doesn't look like it will be dry until Wednesday or so. This is great for me 'cause dad is waitin' for a nice, sunny day to do my bath and the ensuin' haircut! So it's OK by me if it rains 'til Christmas!

Actually, I love the rain and runnin' in it. I love water! It's just when I'm bein' washed and all shampooed up and then sprayed all over that gets me. I even like it when they dry me with that wonderful towel thing. I just get right into it!

I tried to pull what dad called a 'fast-one' yesterday. It was rainin' so hard and I got so wet that I tried to get dad to accept it as the bath part of the groomin'. Dad said, "Nice try, Charley, but the bath is still coming."

Then, guess what I did! Yup, I jumped up in his lap in all my soakin' wetness and licked his face and glasses! I really took him by surprise 'cause it was that really cold, rainy day wetness and it soaked his shorts and he couldn't see out of his glasses! Then, I tried to make my escape but he caught me. Dad sure is quicker than I expect for an old codg … er dad! Then he flipped me on my back and did the tickle-foot grabbin' thing 'cause he knows it drives me nuts! Wow! What a good time!

Mom, of course, was havin' a good laugh over all this. I've made a mental Schnauzer note to get her next time. She was there with the towel to dry me off. I sure love mom 'n dad!

"Recollect that the Almighty, who gave the dog to be companion of our pleasures and our toils, hath invested him with a nature noble and incapable of deceit."

Sir Walter Scott

August 12, 2018

Charley here, friends! I know, I know, ol' motormouth, but I just have to tell you about dad's surprise for me yesterday. Dad said, "c'mon Charley, while mom is out we'll sit out on the side deck and just shoot the breeze. Besides, I have a surprise for you."

So, we go out and sit under the umbrella and dad brings water for me and an iced coffee for himself. No, he didn't serve me what I asked for 'cause he said he was fresh out of bone broth, but I let it slide. It was great just to 'hang out' with dad! After a little small talk about the weather, the Patriots and a little politics, we got to the important stuff, me! Dad asked if I recalled him puttin' me on the table and placin' my foot on a piece of paper? Well, of course I remember! I'm only 11 months old, not 73 years! Oops, sorry, dad! Anyway, I was thinkin' he was measurin' me for some of those human shoe things 'cause I was trackin' dirt in the house.

Well, next thing, dad pulls out this piece of paper and it has my name on it! Dad said it was for me 'cause I can't hold one of those pencil things and I might have to sign my name someday! It is an imprint of my foot with my name on it. WOW! Do I have the best dad, or what? I was so excited I almost had an accident right there at that table. Then dad said he was happy that I was happy! It was like a real love fest!

See ya next time, friends!

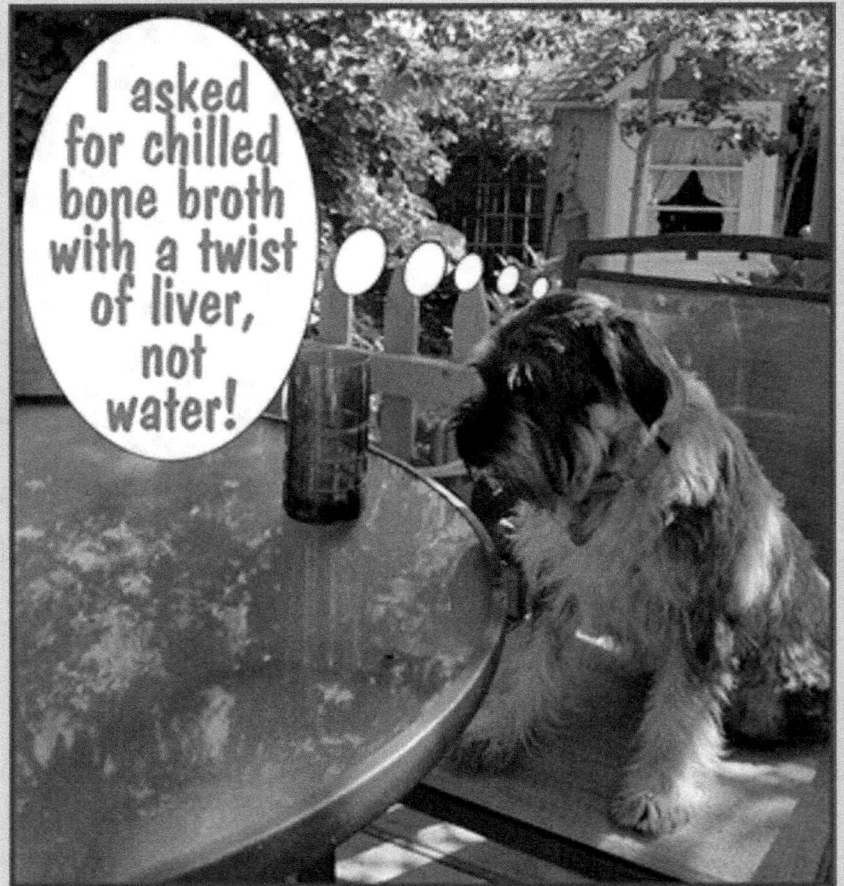

> **After a little small talk about the weather, the Patriots and a little politics, we got to the important stuff, me!**

August 15, 2018

Charley, again! Well, OK, I got into a bit of trouble this morning. It seems like I dug this thing up that I wasn't supposed to. So, there I was, on the back deck, enjoyin' a (finally dry) mornin' and chewin' a newly acquired treasure. Then comes dad with his coffee to sit and check his emails. All of a sudden he yells, in one of those really loud whispers (like he uses when he doesn't want me to wake mom), "OMG! Charley! Where did you find that?" DROP IT! That's a magic wand!

Wow! It was like the old days when I was sure my first name was No and my last name was Drop-it. I'm thinkin', hey, chill, dad! It's only a stick!

Well, I think I've told you before, on the outside, mom 'n dad seem, well … normal. But, at home … look out! It's like they're eatin' kibble that's way past the expiration date! There are a few folks, I hear, that have lived here like Aunty Cheryl, Aunty Tina and Erik that know the truth but they had to sign a non-disclosure thingy, whatever that is!

Anyway, dad picked up the pieces and was gluin' them together inside. I heard him say somethin' to mom about not buryin' it deep enough. Then she asked him, "Charley, (she calls him Charley when she is upset with him) where did you bury the Mandrake root?"

Hmmm? I'm goin' to do some more diggin'!

Magic what?

August 17, 2018

Yeah … Charley here. Just waitin' for dad. He is doin' my bath today. Woe is me.

Sigh …

August 18, 2018

I am STILL waitin' for the bath! It's OK! I've pretty much resigned myself to my fate. I'm actually waitin' in the big water bowl for dad!

But now, friends, I'm kinda lookin' forward to it! Yup, thanks to my friends Demond, Michaela, Deb and especially Kiki, I'm getting' in the zone! I can't wait to spring (or should I say, shake) my surprise for dad!

But while I'm waitin, I thought I would show you a little about where I live, Plum Island and the room dad built in the basement last year where we hang out a lot. They call it Key West. I think it is supposed to be funny. They call our home "Plum Island Paradise". I'm pretty sure they decided that when I got here! Mom says I need to develop a sense of humor cause when I'm older other pups will say she's lovin' and carin' and funny, too! They'll say, "Gimmie four, Charley!"

Oh, by the way, dad says I should ask if any of my friends aren't happy with me postin' this other stuff, just let me know and I'll stop. Yup, friends, don't worry 'bout me! I'll just roll up in a ball and whimper. Just kiddin'!

C'mon dad! I finally got myself psyched-up fer this bath. Here I am in the big drinkin' bowl! Hey, this stuff smells good!

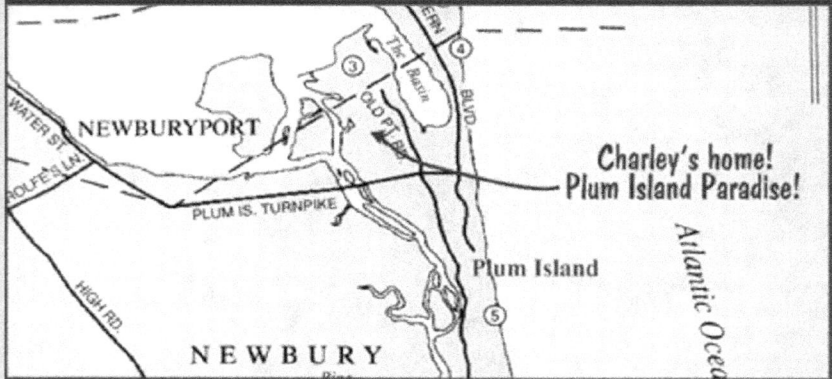

Sign that dad cut out & mom painted!

Where me 'n dad watch the GOAT!

Mini

Dad calls this part of his 'bucket list'!

My Key West bed

Me

NEWBURYPORT

Charley's home! Plum Island Paradise!

PLUM IS. TURNPIKE

Plum Island

Atlantic Ocean

NEWBURY

Our welcome sign goin' home after the bridge!

WELCOME TO PLUM ISLAND

August 19, 2018

OK, friends, you gotta promise to keep this post to yourself! I STILL haven't gotten my bath! I know, right!

So, dad gives me this story about 2 metal knees and it's hard for him to kneel down so it's easier outside. Then he says it's too cold out and he doesn't want me to get a 'chill'! Hey, I'm a Standard Schnauzer! We chill all the time!

Well, you should have seen him when he told me. Charley, he says, there has been a little bump in the road. Hey, friends, dad is 73 years old. His 'road' looks like the one at the hospital with all the speed bumps in it! Dad's 'road' has never been smooth. It's like cobblestones with quite a few missin'.

But dad sure tries hard. When he told me he handed me these things and said, here, wear these until tomorrow! If you don't like your looks, nobody will know who you are!

Hey, friends, I love my looks! It's just that I may be getting' a little over-ripe, if you know what I mean. Maybe I would be better off if dad sprinkled some of his Old Spice on me.

I'll keep you posted!

August 19, 2018

Hi friends. Let's put the bath aside for now 'cause I have a bigger problem!

With my 1st birthday comin' on Sept. 1st, I have to polish up my guardin' skills. Ideally, I want the pack to be together … always! But mom 'n dad keep throwin' me off balance. We'll all be in the kitchen. Then mom goes one way to her studio and dad goes upstairs to work on the computer, or he goes downstairs to his shop. What is a little girl Standard Schnauzer protector supposed to do? For now, I lay on the landing between up 'n down and just keep my ears open. But, if one of them goes off in the car, I'm just beside myself 'til they get back and we are a pack again.

The other thing is when mom 'n dad might be close, or huggin' I seem to just want to jump up between them. Of course, they laugh and don't get mad at me but, I don't know what it is. I just can't help myself.

Oh, well, just wanted to get that off my chest. Dad says that on weekends I have way too much time on my hands! Gotta go! Dad's makin' meatloaf!

August 19, 2018

I know, I know, 3 in one day! Dad says I'm getting' to be a real motor-mouth, whatever that is. BUT, I had to tell you, we have finally settled the bath thing!

I summoned up my whole 11-month self and had a heart-to-heart with mom 'n dad! I told dad that things were so bad the little critters are smellin' me comin' first. I told him that I am runnin' into walls 'cause my beard is getting' in my eyes

So, dad said he would give me a bath tomorrow, somehow, and mom promised that if the weather doesn't cooperate, then she will bathe me in the tub. Then, dad can do my haircut, no problem, 'cause of the special thingy he built in the basement.

Friends, next time you hear from me I'll be one happy puppy! BTW, girlfriends, what is this stuff I hear mom talkin' about called lipstick?

Mom! Don't tell dad but, ya gotta help me. Girl to girl, mom, you know I NEED this bath!

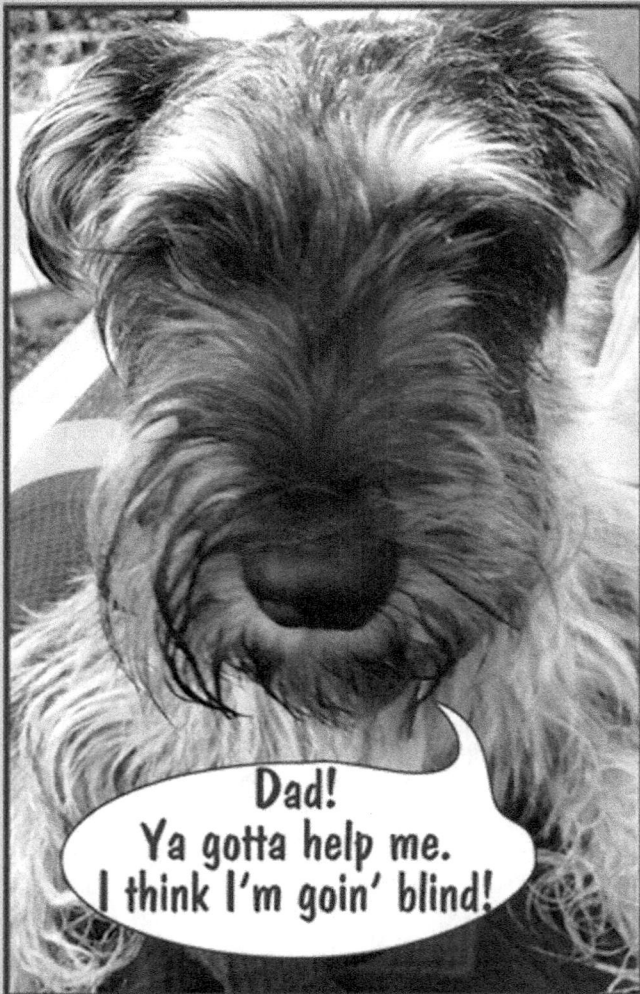

Dad! Ya gotta help me. I think I'm goin' blind!

Wait ... what? No dad, I don't recall sayin' a thing to mom regarding you or that green thing over there.

Green thing!

August 20, 2018

Well, my wonderful friends, it's over! Mom 'n dad gave me my bath today, outside, at our Plum Island Paradise! I really want to thank everyone for their comments and suggestions, especially the one about getting' dad wet! That worked like a charm! I even heard him mumble somethin' to mom about getting' more of a bath than Charley did. Tee hee hee.

Dad, wait! I've changed my mind about all this bath stuff!

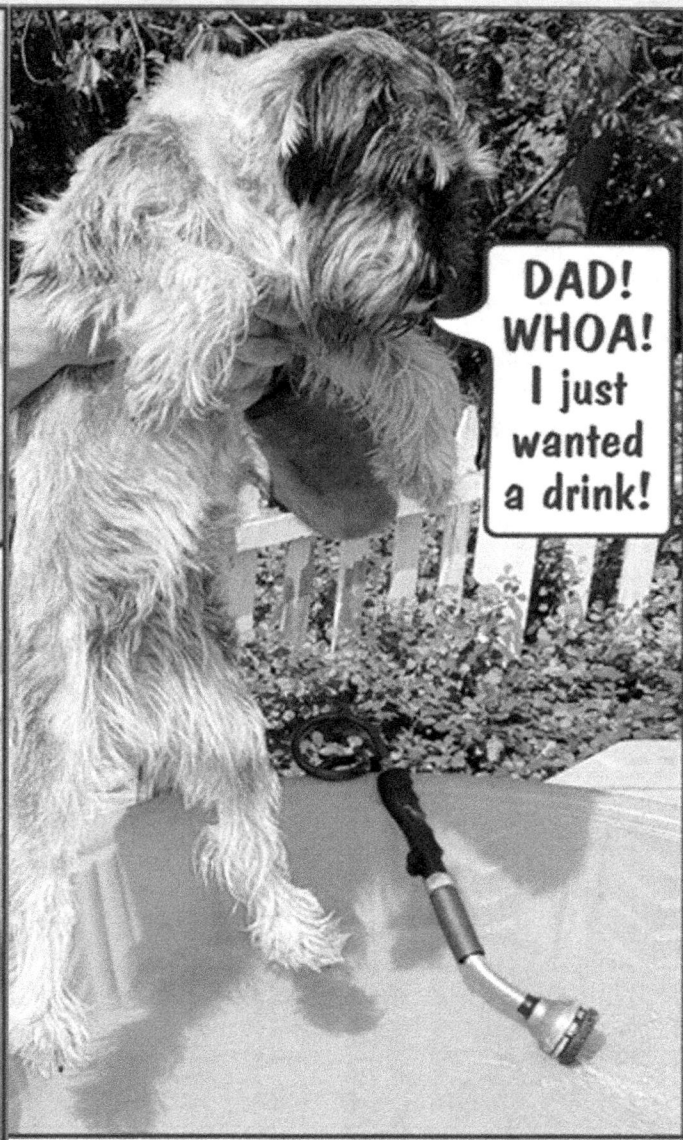

DAD! WHOA! I just wanted a drink!

When dad said Earthbath, I'm thinkin' mud roll!

Now, I just want to set the record straight … I was NOT concerned one little bit about that silly ol' bath. I was just havin' some fun, yeah, that's it, I was pullin' your leg! Also, if you ever hear any gossip that may originate right here in Paradise, don't you believe it! Especially if it contains a phrase I heard dad whisperin' to mom, 'drama queen'! I don't think it means royalty, so it isn't me!

Then there are these pictures. Now, don't get me wrong, I appreciate that mom took them but I made the big mistake of askin' dad to put the captions on them 'cause I was really busy with a bully stick dad gave me as a special treat après le bain. Dad says that means 'after the bath' in French but, for all I know, it could mean 'kick me'!

Anyway, pay no attention to the captions! Bye, see you after my haircut, tomorrow!

There, Charley, It's all over.

Hey! No worries!

When dad gets me dry I see where that hose thingy is and I'm gonna have some fun!

August 21, 2018

Hi, friends. It's really me, Charley! I feel like I have to get a tattoo or somethin' so you will recognize me! Dad finished part 1 of my haircut and he is givin' me a break & a treat so I will like the experience. Between you 'n me, I think dad is the one needin' the break!

OMG, I'm naked! Dad's not finished yet 'cause he likes to give me a break, but OMG!

OMG, AGAIN! Does anyone have some glue? I feel like somebody should say a few of them poignant words!

Besides, 'member I told you about his artificial knees? Well, he also gets a needle in his eye every month, so I'm hopin' for the best. I'll tell you though when he's wavin' them clippers, I keep my eyes closed and my ears 'n tail tucked way in! Dad took a picture of me to this point but I cropped it. A girl should only show her best side, you know. Anyway, I'll be back when dad is through, but first, we have to pick up mom and have lunch. Bye!

August 21, 2018

Hi, friends. New Charley here!

So dad finished my doo today. He says he still wants to do a couple of spots but that I was getting' antsy! I don't know what antsy means but I'm sure I wasn't doin' it! Anyway, when dad put me down he said, "Phew! That's that for another year!" He was smirkin' so I know he was kiddin'!

Well, I ran to the upstairs bath mirror, bein that's the only one I can see myself in, and I was shocked! Shocked, I tell you! First of all, I look like I lost 10 pounds! Not only that, I looked naked!

I ran down to dad and told him I didn't look like my Schnauzer friends who win prizes 'n stuff. I asked him

I wonder if dad asked about that lipstick stuff?

if they will still want to be my friends.

Charley, he said, you are beautiful and mom 'n me love you no matter how you look. As for your friends, they know more than most that it's not looks that make a Standard Schnauzer, it's what is in their heart, and you, Charley, are 110% Schnauzer! Then dad did my favorite thing with the ticklin' my belly and we laughed 'til our sides hurt and there were tears in our eyes. Wow! Life is good!

> **" Then dad did my favorite thing with the ticklin' my belly and we laughed 'til our sides hurt and there were tears in our eyes. Wow! Life is good! "**

August 23, 2018

Hi friends, Charley here.

First of all, there is no beach time for Charley! Yeah, there is somethin' called sharks over there and dad says we have to stay outa the water. WAIT! … what? It's just a big fish, right? I can't figure these humans out!

Well, I'm sure glad that bath 'n haircut is over with. I guess there were a few things they call 'matts' in my beard so dad is now on a mission to keep me brushed. Seems like every minute I see him reach for that torture thing and come at me. I've kinda resigned myself to my fate now and just let him brush me.

WEATHER
Today:
Mostly sunny;
nice, less humid.
High of 77.
Tonight:
Low of 57.
Page 24

The DAILY NEWS

WWW.NEWBURYPORTNEWS.COM
THURSDAY
August 23, 2018
$1.50

New England Newspaper & Press Association's 2017 Newspaper of the Year

Local anglers spot sharks off Plum Island

By Jack Shea

How come he gets so fiesty when dad's holdin' 'im?

Honest, mom, I didn't hurt 'im! He's been like a limp, rag doll ever since dad brought 'im home!

So, with the shark thing and all we are just hangin' out at our Plum Island Paradise, (well, just forget the shark thing!), and I'm tryin' to engage the old timers in some fun 'n games. I grabbed fox but I have to be careful 'cause of an incident a while ago with a fox that ain't with us any longer. Luckily, they fell for the story that I was tryin' to resuscitate him when they found us!

Oh, BTW, mom 'n dad were, I think they said, floored, yesterday 'cause dad told me to go get fox. So, I went into the other room 'n got him and brought him back to dad. I thought he was gonna fall out of his chair. He had a long discussion with mom, like, OMG, how does she know that? Then they did the same thing with my Rumba bone today. I went 'n got it! What's the big deal? Humans!

"The dog was created specially for children. He is the god of frolic."

Henry Ward Beecher

August 24, 2018

Hi, everybody! I had a great day today. I helped dad put up a new shelf and lights for mom's studio and she was really happy when she came home from teachin' her art class!

The best part, though, was that I got to go to my human brother Erik's house for dinner and to show off my new doo! My sister-in-law Tanya was there and cousin Kate. I was sad that my cousin Kyle wasn't there 'cause he is learnin' to be a flyboy in the Air Force. Their Yellow Lab, Kodi, stayed upstairs, I think 'cause he had a headache.

Anyway, it was a wonderful time and I got to play with everyone and dad slipped me a couple pieces of meat from the grill, under the table!

'Night, friends. I'm goin' to sleep it off!

> Oh, Kate, oh wonderful cousin Kate! Are you goin' to eat that terrible piece of meat on your plate? I'll be glad to help. Kate ... Kate?

> I am soo trying to ignore those two crazies!

> Give me some beef, Erik or I swear, I'll honk your nose again!

August 25, 2018

> C'mon, seagulls, I just want to be friends!

Dad's seagull.

The weekend is off to a good start, friends. It was a great visit last night and this mornin' I'm chillin' with mom 'n dad.

But, I have a question for my four-legged pals out there, how do you deal with them bird things? I mean, usually, it's just them little flittin' things that are just distractin' and the occasional hawk or eagle who won't even give ya the time of day! No, I'm talkin' about the two that drive me nuts. They are called seagulls and the black seagulls dad calls crows. I'm tellin' ya, they just yell at me but won't engage!

I know about seagulls 'cause dad did a pastel of one a long time ago. Mom is really the artist (I'm talkin' pro, big time artist) but dad just dabbles! Forty years ago, when dad met mom, he didn't know about Plum Island, bein' from a place called the Bronx 'n all. But mom grew up here, and when she met dad she told him it was a requirement to learn to draw seagulls to live on Plum Island!

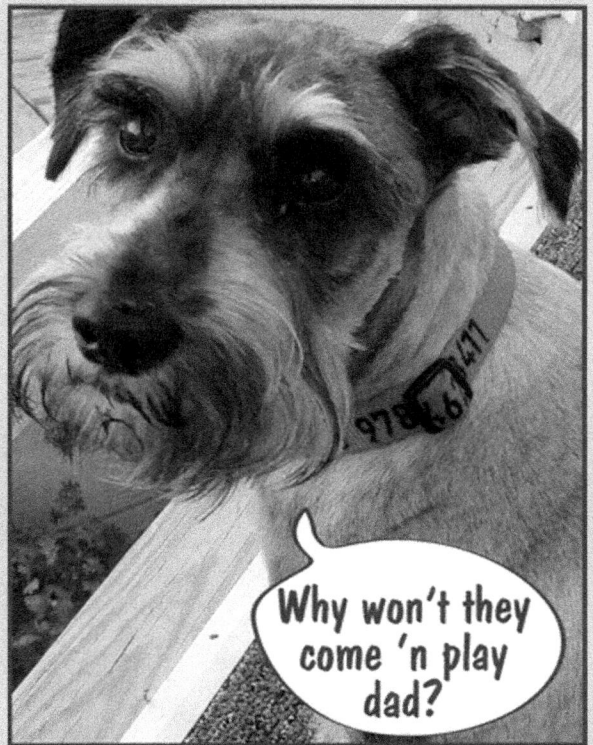

> Why won't they come 'n play dad?

Uh, oh! Here they come! I might get in trouble again for makin' stuff up. Gotta go!

August 27, 2018

Well, let me tell you, I had the best dog-gone time yesterday! We went to a place called New Hampshire to visit my cousin Augie and, oh, yeah, my human cousins too! (just kiddin'). Trisha and Chris were there and their liter, Emma and Eliza! It's kind of funny that humans don't seem to distribute their pups like we do. Anyway, I'm glad 'cause I had a lot of fun with them, especially Emma & Eliza!

Anyway, it was a nice family get together. Trisha was shuckin' corn for dinner, Chris was hidin' a marmot from me (that's a big squirrel), and Augie and I played a lot, although I was a little upset when she blew the whistle on me and my escape attempt!

My auntie Tina was there too cause they were havin' a birthday get together for her. BTW, it's MY birthday in a few days!

It was sure an excitin' day and dad said I looked tired when we got back to our Plum Island Paradise. I told him that I was in no way tired and ready for more fun. Then he took a pic to prove me wrong! Oh, well. See you soon!

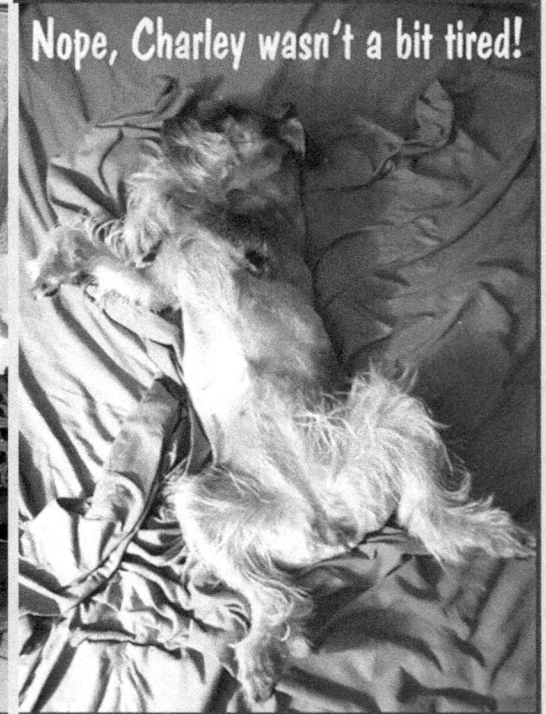

August 28, 2018

Hi friends, it's what's left of Charley here! Dad wouldn't take me with him today 'cause he said it was 100 degrees when he went to do errands this afternoon. And the index (whatever that is) was 106 degrees. All I know is that it was HOT! Dad keeps makin' sure there is cold water in my bowl and he put the fan in the kitchen where I like to be, by the door, waitin' for him 'n mom to come home! Wow, my mom 'n dad sure do take care of me!

So, I pretty much stayed near the computer today, cleanin' up some things and workin' on this post. Dad said he spoke to someone at the grocery store and my name came up. Seems like dad nonchalantly asked the other dog owner how often her dog posts on Facebook. Well, that started it! After a while she said, "Wait,… what? You're tryin' to tell me your Schnauzer does her own posts?"

Dad said he started to 'splain but realized it was useless to describe our symbiotic relationship. That's why, when I needed his help, he decided to take my picture at the computer.

> No, dad! Not my picture! You know I need help doin' the Ctrl + C on the keyboard!

Of course, I was actually usin' mom's computer today. That's why you can't see my 'big paws' keyboard and my non-edible mouse! Dad says he made my computer desk out of a dogwood tree, but I don't believe him 'cause mom gave me the 'look' when he said it.

Stay cool, friends and I'll see ya soon!

August 29, 2018

Hi, friends! It sure has been hot, hasn't it? I hope all my doggy friends are remindin' your significant others to give you plenty of cold water, shade and maybe an ice cube or two! No, I didn't say ice cream! Don't go getting' me into trouble!

So, dad 'n me went to pick up mom last night. We get there a little early so I can see my Tuesday night paintin' girls. But, when we got there, some were gone already, like Lisa, Linda and Mary! I hated missin' them!

Anyway, Kathy & Tina were still there and Tina had a present for dad. I know, I know, I usually get the presents but I'm gonna be a year old on Saturday and I might get a present then.

Well, when dad opened his present, it looked like I felt when I got all those pills for my getting' fixed pain! It was an apron ('cause the girls know dad does the cookin') and it had a Schnauzer picture on it. It said, "My Schnauzer Colors My World"! Dad sure was happy to get it. I think he even looked like he does when we watch those sad movies on the picture thing. Glad we got a picture with me, Tina, Kathy 'n dad!

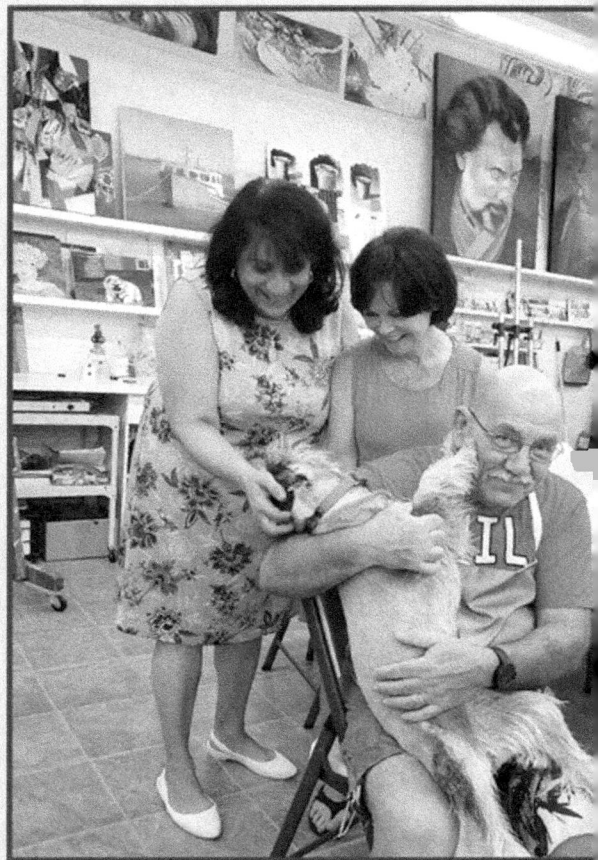

August 30, 2018

Mom! Don't distract me! Dad says I have to watch them guys with the fence!

Hi friends, Charley again!

I've been tryin' to walk the straight 'n narrow with my birthday comin' in two days. I don't want to rock the boat here at our Plum Island Paradise and maybe miss out on a present or somethin'! Dad hasn't said anythin' but I saw him talkin' hush-hush to mom, if you know what I mean.

So, dad gives me assignments and I am doin' my best to guard stuff. Today, I'm supposed to keep an eye on the new neighbors who are puttin' up a fence for their two dogs. Dad says, like all Standard Schnauzers, I'm exceptional at noticin' and awareness. He says he could swap two pictures on the wall and I would notice right away!

Dad, I'm outta here! I know you're in charge, but I just can't stand you flauntin' the authority thing!

Well, things were goin' real good this mornin', that is until dad came out with his mornin' coffee and that obnoxious shirt he was wearin'! Hello! Can you say, Rub-It-In? Dad says Lucy never minded it but, hey dad, there's a new kid in town! I mean, I'll accept it, but I ain't havin' it put up in lights! I need a shirt that says, "BETTA FEMALE"! See ya next time, friends!

August 31, 2018

Charley here, friends!

Well, I had to show my tough side today. Mom was over talkin' to the new neighbor and her two labs. I wasn't very happy about that and I yelled at those two to make sure they kept their distance from mom! I haven't met them yet and I insist on doin' a 'background check' (if you know what I mean) before they can get chummy with mom!

Then my day changed completely when mom 'n dad 'n me met my cousin Danyelle and her pup Chewy. Danyelle says that it is short for his real name, Chewbacca!

We met at the art studio 'cause they thought it would be more room to run around. Whoa! This is the first time I've met a pup younger than me by 4 months and OMG! They don't call him Chewy for nothin'! Danyelle thinks he is part Beagle and somethin' else. Personally, I think he is part Piranha. Hmmm? Now that I think about it, dad used to say that very same thing about me!

Anyway, I loved meetin' cousin Danyelle and Chewy. We had lots of fun slidin' from one end of the studio to the other and dodgin' those table legs! Thanks for installin' such a nice, slippery floor, dad.

I'm gonna cut this short 'cause I am fallin' asleep at the computer and I expect a big day tomorrow, bein it's my birthday!

Wow! I forgot what it was like to be 8 months old!

CHAPTER 12

September 1, 2018

Whoopie!!! Whoopie!!! Everybody. I am 1 year old today!

Yup, Charley here, friends, and I am announcin' my retirement from puppyhood. I know, dad says I'm still gonna have a lot of my puppy traits for a while yet, but I am ready for the big time!

I was so excited this mornin' that I woke dad up extra early. I licked him a couple times and when he opened his eyes, there I was, sayin', "Come on lazy bones, it's my birthday!" So, we got up and commiserated for a while and then took mom to work. We went back to pick mom up and had lunch and then, a surprise birthday party. I was floored, I tell you. There were party favors and a birthday brownie, a free birthday present from Quinn's Canine Café!

Mom 'n dad got me a new collar that they said is black with bling on it but it was bark-ordered! I'll post a pic when it finally comes. I sure am happy today!

I'm gonna go eat some more brownie 'n play all day! Bye, my friends. I'll be thinkin' of you!

Epilogue: Time to Fess Up!

You are probably asking yourself, "Could this possibly be true?" We know Charley can write, but, can she truly write such accomplished humor at mere months of age? Could this Standard Schnauzer really compose Facebook posts that leave us laughing so hard we are left standing in a puddle of tears? Might she be the first *Human Whisperer*?

Well, I am Charley's dad and I am here to tell you there is no question in my mind! Hmmm, maybe that should be the end of this epilogue but ... but ... she will not ALLOW IT!

The reason is that in the past 10 months, Charley has completely invaded my mind! I mean, c'mon friends, we know the Schnauzer can't actually *type on the keyboard*, right? No, she makes me do it! I don't, for the life of me, know how she seems to control me but all of a sudden she is in my head ... or am I in *her* head? It doesn't matter. All I know is that I am suddenly sitting here typing her thoughts and taking her pictures like she is in control of me.

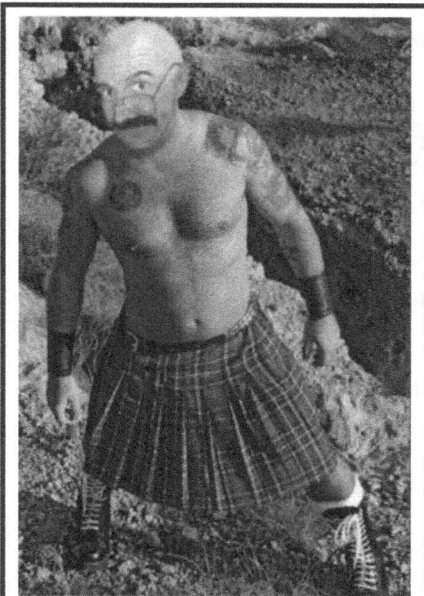

Charley discovered I was Scottish and made me do this picture.

To have fun, she makes me portray myself as all these figures. Then she says, no wonder I'm strange, look what kind of dad I have! So, Charley says it is my doing but I, DAD, a human being, a rational adult, a person who, until a year ago was as straight-laced as they come, tell you it is 100% Charley's doing!

It hasn't always been this way. I remember the first day when we absorbed Charley into our lives. She was the perfect Schnauzerism, a bundle of pepper & salt hair, cuddled like crazy and peed in the car.

In all fairness, Charley had very few accidents. Because we got her in November, at the start of a harsh winter, coupled with the fact that our home isn't very conducive to whisking a puppy outside 84 times a day, we went the training pad route. Charley grasped the idea immediately and, while she didn't have trouble finding the pad, her aim left a little to be desired. Let me put it this way, had she been a bombardier in WWII, she may have hit Wyoming! She simply assumed if her feet were touching the pad, she was good to go, literally! She never made the slightest connection that the 'action end' would itself, be best located over the pad!

Then there was the BFA on our part. That stands for Bodily Function Awareness. It goes like this. You see a pup do her business in the yard and think, isn't it cute, that little trickle. But, when it happens inside, on the pad, and you go to pick it up, you are certain that pad came pre-loaded with dried pee that was activated when little Charley hit it! Hello! Where in God's name does it all come from? Those pads are advertised to hold, like a pint of fluid. Well Charley must pee a *quart* at a time! It never failed to impress. Every time we pick up what seemed like, 20 pounds of pad, there was Lake Michigan under it.

Getting back to how Charley sees us, well, it's not pretty, folks. We are just your everyday, fun loving couple. I have always been a rather serious man who doesn't really want to call attention to himself, as you can see from the pictures below.

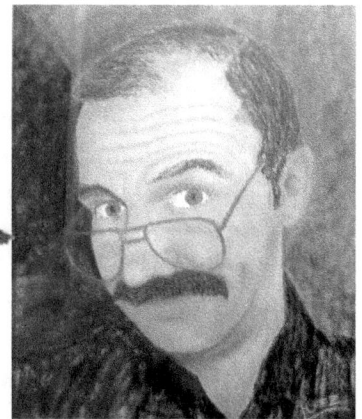

These pictures of me (dad), are pretty indicative of my serious nature. They are also indicative of my unrivaled artistic talents because I made them ... NOT Charley, as much as she would like to take credit for them! I'm sure you have noticed throughout these posts that Charley has insinuated, if not outright said, that SHE is responsible for some artwork. Please don't believe her! Charley, as much as some of you may not believe it, does not have opposable thumbs! I do admit, however, to tying markers to her paw so she could do the cartoons of me.

Below, you will see a picture of Pat (mom) and me (dad) as we truly are; no nonsense, down-to-earth, regular, God fearing folks.

OK! I confess, we don't really have much use for a pitchfork here at out Plum Island Paradise, but you have to admit, it adds a nice, homey touch.

So, now that you know who the 'real' mom and dad are, I would surely appreciate your not being quite so gullible when Charley makes me portray us as some other weird characters. For instance, in a recent Q & A that Charley graciously participated in with some online magazine that follows her posts, (like, why do they want *her* opinion?), she was asked to describe mom and dad. She decided to send them some pictures

she dug up on MY computer. Hello! Can you say 'out of context'? This is what she sent for mom. And, if you think

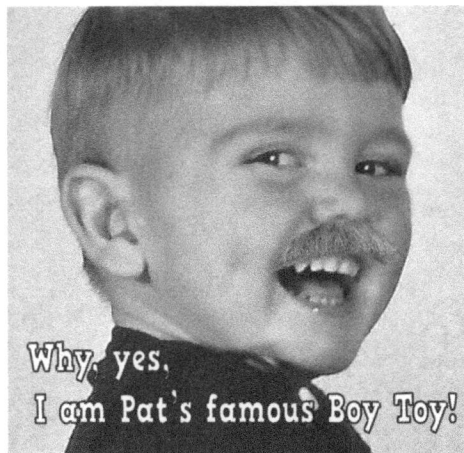

Why, yes, I am Pat's famous Boy Toy!

that's bad, here are the pictures that Charley sent to represent me! The first she says is me as a kid! Hey, can you say Photoshop? Then she says she wanted to show I'm not perfect, so she sent this one that was taken

because Lucy didn't have a license! We were framed. Lucy wasn't even driving! As you saw in Charley's post, she is making me wear her license now. Finally, Charley

tell you! I do NOT have curly hair!

I realize now that it was a mistake to give her access to my files! She keeps finding these crazy pictures, pictures that, for the most part, I have no recollection of their context.

For instance, this picture of Billy the Kid. Did we fake this picture or, or, could this be one of my ancestors? I just don't know, I tell you. I'm 73 and losing it!

I do, however recall this image. For a while I was doing a graphic design business at our art school and this was my logo. Hmmm, no wonder I'm not in that business now!

But, do you see what I mean? I had no intention of showing this picture and there it is. It is like she kidnaps my fingers and makes them do things as I watch, sometimes in horror!

And then there is this one! OMG! I can't even begin to imagine what the occasion was. Was it Halloween? Was I being punish for some crazy stunt I was framed for? Who

knows? I'm telling you, this Standard Schnauzer, this little girl, this puppy is undoubtedly proof that they are the dog with the human brain!

As a final example, I'll show you 3 more that she "says" she found buried in the bowels of my computer! Just look at these! How incongruous can you

get? Is she saying I'm a bunny, a crook or a philosopher? Oh, pu-lease, give me a break!

Well, here is a final one that I do happen to remember. It was my beautiful bride, Pat's first attempt at a clay figure. It was on our kitchen table while she worked on it and actually scared me a couple of times when I came down for breakfast. Personally, I think she did a great job. I guess if you are an artist, you are an artist, no matter what the medium.

So, I'm leaving you with this ... when all is said and done, don't believe a word of what that little Charley says!

This is what c.f. lutz really looks like!

COMMENTS

Charley's friends on Facebook have been awesome!
They have stood by her throughout her first year and have lovingly taken the time to offer advice, encouragement and support. There have been so many comments that it would be impossible to list them all so, if you do not see yours please understand. We sincerely appreciate every comment, love, like, laugh, surprise and sorrow you have taken the time to send.

Betsy:
- Oh Charley, I am so glad Dad saw what you brought in! We would miss seeing you here if you got sick!
- Oh Charley..you could not get any "cooler"!

Cari:
- My previous SS Lewis always split the difference and found a mid way spot. My new guy Jackson, doesn't seem to be worked up about this, at all! LOL

Carol:
- Charley, Charley, Charley... never try to play Rope a Dope with an older dog, they're very experienced... • Memorize this adage: "OId age and treachery will always beat youth and exuberance"

Catherine:
- Hi Charley, Dash here. I'm new to the group. Sorry for your troubles. Some dogs are just grumpy fun police. I think we live close enough to each other for a play date. You're on Plum Island right? I live over by the Artichoke. Be fun to play with another Schnauzer who knows how to romp and roll!!

Darcy:
- LMAO! Great rendition of a traumatic event. So glad your mom and dad let you use the computer so you could tell us about it. I'm gonna tell Miss Zoey and Miss Jackie to watch out for that Shephard ...he's got bad manners!

Deb:
- Charley is absolutely adorable!! And you have a wonderful sense of humor! Love Charley's point of view. LOL
- Kiki says she feels your pain but look at it this way as much as u rock the scruffy look, you will have every one going Gaga over you when you are well groomed. So suck it up and enjoy the results. At least that is what my mama tells me.
- Kiki says, " you go girl show 'em what Schnauzers are made of we are not aftaid of a little ol' bath, besides you will look beautiful!". And my Mama says please dont stop posting she loves them and reads them to me! We love your sense of humor.
- Oh, Charley love the shades! Not showing this to Kiki or she will want a pair.
- You are doing great Charlie , you remind me of Kiki at that age. I always look forward to your posts so keep 'em coming!

DeeDe:
- Ah, Charley, life will never be boring for your mom and dad hoping you heal quickly and stay away from the business end of other, less than friendly pups.

Denise:
- Lol lol lol, adorable, this really made me laugh. Great sense of humor, Charley has taught you well, lol

Diane:
- Always a great way to start the day, reading a post from you Charley!
- Charley, don't spit the pills out! You need to get better, so you can keep writing your posts...what would we do without them? Get better soon!
- Charley, I am going to post a pic of Denny Lee, my 10 month old male. You two would make a great pair, it's just too bad we live far away on Vancouver Island.

• Charley, you are funny. I look forward to seeing your posts and reading all about you. I hope my 8 month old SS grows up to be just like you!

• I hope you are going to put a book together of all your posts. They really are the best! I have a 8month old male SS so I can compare the things they both do. Of course, I am no where near as funny as you!

• I LOVE when your posts show up, I get such a kick out of them. What an awesome girl you are Miss Charley!

• Please don't ever stop Charley. I love your posts and look forward to reading them every time, as I'm sure everyone does. You are a funny, beautiful girl with a dad that has a great sense of humor. Your posts are the best!

• Oh Charley, you are the best. I love, love, love your posts. I am going to put out our big "water bowl" for Denny and see if he loves it as much as you (but I will close the door first!). Have a wonderful day. Aparna ML I love reading about your adventures Charlie! Can't wait to hear all about your next venture!

• Sorry you got hurt, but your stories are told so well and are so funny, they make my day. Now stay away from the big boys!

Gale:

• Sorry Charley, but your mean look needs some work. You are just too cute so it won't come easy!!

Gerry:

  • A book, please! These postings are great.

Gisele:

• Love your stuff! Keep Charley busy with his adventures.

• You are beautiful to me....there is something wonderful about your natural look...you should see my Sergeant

• Pepper and I think he looks great!

Jennifer 1:

• Charley- Faith says she has the same problem! When her Mom and Dad get close, SHE also feels the impulsive drive to get between them!

• I love it when dogs puff up their cheeks when they smile Charlie - you are so pretty

• Oh Charley you little stinker. Charlotte and Faith recommend Greenies pill pockets - they taste like yummy treats and you can't taste the pill.

Jennifer 2:

• Wait, Charlie is a girl?!?!

• This just totally changes the voice in my head as I read her posts!

Jona:

• Hi Charley, my name is Lola. I tried asking for an iPad, but mom said no. Maybe your Dad will get one for you? They are especially fun to watch the pictures change when you lick the screen!

Julia:

• I know im biased and ive got 2 minis as well as a standard but there's no cuddle like a Standard schnauzer head cuddle and Charley your cute face just melts me.

Kate:

• Oh Charley, you imp! When I head to Plum Island this fall, I will bring Zivah with me to say hello - Abby is going to go have a big adventure soon, so she won't be able to go.

Marcia:

• Charley you're such a scamp!

• Any time Charley! That's what I love about you SS. Sounds like your Mom and Dad get a lot of entertainment value from you and I enjoy your posts.

• Charlie can't wait to see your new doo, you'll be even more handsome if that's even possible.

• My parents won't let me chase any birds. They ruin all my fun except squirrels and chipmunks. Mea

Margo:

• Give em hell Charley! Just stand your ground stand fast do not move anywhere when asked or they try to move you! Hide your face do not look up no matter what! Do not allow him near your ears or your butt! Butt protection sit down and refuse to get up! Do not offer any help what so over and you can sue em for all sorts of stuff they do to you against your will! You go girl! Show em who's boss!

Michaela:
  • Hi Charley, this is Hugo - have to tell you that I have trained my mom into not getting a nervous breakdown everytime I go on patrol in the neighborhood. It took me almost 2 years, but now she is OK with me going out to check whether it is safe for anyone to go out of their houses. I enjoy it very much and it only takes 11 minutes (according to what my mom tells her friends). So girl, do not despair - some people can be somewhat difficult to work with. Best regards, Hugo.
  • Charley, you are just great - love Reading about your adventures.
  • Charley, you are one heck of a girl - typical SS in every thinkable way - remind me of one of my earlier SS who ate rat poison; Believe me, it was more than scary. But he did well and after a while I recovered, too. Hoping you will eat the pill for the time necessary and that dad will put the poison somewhere where you absolutely cannot reach it. Take care, all of you.
  • Hey Charley, Hugo and Kajsa asked me to tell you that these birds are a nuisance whether on the ground or flying. However, you do the right thing - Watch them and stand your ground. (One never knows) Also, appreciate your mom and dad, as they are giving you numerous opportunities to explore the World and eberything in it. Have a faboulous weekend.
  • Well, Charley - this greeting from Kajsa and Hugo is only to remind you that it takes a great deal of work to train your mom and dad - owners of SS do very often have a lot in common with their dogs. From your comments I can read that you are well on the way - so keep up the good work and remind yourself that only when being persistant, you will succeed. Good luck from all 3 of us.:)

Patricia:
  • I look forward to your posts love hearing about your antics Charley and yes u do live in paradise Plum Island is a magical place so lucky.

Ret:
  • Beautiful. But it made me cry and miss my Pippa but I'll never forget that unconditional love. Never.
  • Oh Charley you big silly. You big silly gorgeous girl who will one day read the signs of the barks and growls.
  • Poor Charley everyone thinks you're a boy but you're too gorgeous for a boy and obviously a girl.
  • There's nothing better than a schnauzer snuggle. Oh how I miss my Pippa snuggles. Charley is beautiful and growing fast.

Teresa:
  • Dang Charlie we love your posts... You and dad have a great day.
  • Don't every stop posting Charley Porter and Shandey and their other siblings love when I read them your posts... PS I love your stories too

Tina:
  • Charley your new do is very fashionable and chic, just right for a beautiful young lady, just keep that wiggle under control around the boy schnauzers!

Charley Toons

So, you may be saying to yourself ...

Wait ... what!

Believe me, we here at Plum Island Communications are with you, but we can explain!

You see, when Charley's birthday was fast approaching on September 1st, we realized there would not be enough pages for a spine! Yup, you read correctly. Who wants a spineless story book?

Just picture it. You've spent good money for Charley's hilarious Facebook posts, you put it on your shelf because you simply can't continue to laugh like this or you may break something. The next day you go for Charley and you sit in your recliner and realize it is the printer manual, or the local guide to bird species in your town or, your MMPI test from 1976! That's what happens with spineless books, they blend!

We couldn't possibly let that happen, so we added a few pages to be thick enough for a spine!

Why these kinds of pages, you ask? Frankly, we don't know. We thought of recipes for dog food or even some of those dog-gone Snoopy comics but we decided to keep it about ... who? Yeah ... Charley!

So, you can let the kids color them, frame a couple for your dog's doghouse or shred them and add it to your pups kibble. Be forwarned, though, if you do that your canine may start doing some 'funny' stuff.

PLUM ISLAND MA

Lutz

Lutz

Lutz

Lutz

Pssssst! Don't make this a dog-eared book! Use this page for notes!

Examples:

✓ Don't forget to order 20 30 copies of this hilarious book for all of my dog loving friends!

✓ Email author (c.f. lutz) at:

charleyss@comcast.net, and give him feedback.

www.ingramcontent.com/pod-product-compliance
Lightning Source LLC
La Vergne TN
LVHW080145090426
835509LV00038BA/1574